# CORPORATE SOCIAL AWARENESS AND FINANCIAL OUTCOMES

## Ahmed Riahi-Belkaoui

**QUORUM BOOKS**
Westport, Connecticut • London

**Library of Congress Cataloging-in-Publication Data**

Riahi-Belkaoui, Ahmed, 1943–
    Corporate social awareness and financial outcomes / Ahmed Riahi-
Belkaoui.
        p.   cm.
    Includes bibliographical references and index.
    ISBN 1–56720–243–8 (alk. paper)
    1. Social responsibility of business.   2. Social accounting.
    3. Environmental auditing.   4. Organizational effectiveness.
    I. Title.
    HD60.R52   1999
    658.4'08—dc21          98–34291

British Library Cataloguing in Publication Data is available.

Library of Congress Catalog Card Number: 98–34291
ISBN: 1–56720–243–8

First published in 1999

Quorum Books, 88 Post Road West, Westport, CT 06881
An imprint of Greenwood Publishing Group, Inc.

Printed in the United States of America

The paper used in this book complies with the
Permanent Paper Standard issued by the National
Information Standards Organization (Z39.48–1984).

10 9 8 7 6 5 4 3 2 1

To my family: here and everywhere

# Contents

# Exhibits

# Preface

With calls for social awareness rising against the selfish tide of un-
checked capitalism, most corporations have responded with various
forms of "environmental accounting" and "measures of corporate effectiveness." The financial outcomes to both attempts are the best measures of success. Accordingly, this book entitled *Corporate Social
Awareness and Financial Outcomes* evaluates both environmental accounting and corporate effectiveness (chapter 1) and evaluates the financial outcomes as follows:

1. Economic performance and corporate effectiveness (chapter 2).

2. Air pollution as an example of social cost (chapter 3).

3. CEO compensation and corporate effectiveness (chapter 4).

4. Asset management performance and corporate effectiveness
   (chapter 5).

5. Financial determinants of the decision to disclose social information (chapter 6).

6. User reaction to environmental accounting (chapter 7).

7. Market reaction to environmental accounting (chapter 8).

8. Financial determinants of the extent of environmental disclosure (chapter 9).

This book should be of interest to accounting practitioners, chief financial officers, and other executives, as well as to undergraduate and graduate students of social accounting.

Many people helped in the development of this book. I received considerable assistance from the University of Illinois at Chicago research assistants, especially Belia Ortega. I also thank Eric Valentine, Rebecca Ardwin, and the entire production team at Quorum Books for their continuous and intelligent support. Finally, to Hédi and Janice, thanks for making everything possible and enjoyable.

# 1 _____

# Corporate Social Awareness: The Issues

## INTRODUCTION

Through their corporate social awareness actions, firms signal to the market their willingness to act as good citizens. The methods used are numerous, but they generally fall into the three categories of

a) adopting techniques of *socio-economic accounting*,

b) insuring adequate *corporate reputation*, and,

c) eliminating *fraudulent practices*.

These three categories are the subject of this chapter. Each of these three concepts needs to be well explicated for a better implementation by firms and for a better measurement and assessment of the financial outcomes following this adoption.

## SOCIO-ECONOMIC ACCOUNTING

### Definition of Socio-Economic Accounting

Socio-economic accounting as a term and as a subdiscipline of accounting is a relatively new phenomenon. It is sometimes confused with social accounting, which is an established field of accounting and economics. Social accounting was first introduced by J. R. Hicks of Oxford University in *The Social Framework: An Introduction to Economics*, published in 1942.[1] The accounting research of the time interpreted it as the whole system of accounts and balance sheets of a nation or a region, the price and quantity components of these accounts, and the various considerations to be derived therefrom.[2] Social accounting was basically associated with national income accounting. An examination of the early publications in the accounting literature proves that point. A general theme in the early literature is the failure of the accountant to be involved in social accounting.[3,4]

There were few noticeable involvements of accountants in the area of social accounting. The American Accounting Association, for example, created a Committee on National Income, which issued a report in 1952 on Aspects of National Income. The members of this committee worked on independent projects of their own choosing. Notable examples include "The Classification of Sector in the Social Accounts," by Julius Margolis, and "Use of Accounting Data in National Income Estimation," by Carl L. Nelson.[5] Other attempts examined the role of accountants in social accounting.[6] M. E. Murphy summarizes this role as follows:

> A system of social accounts provides an historical record of a country's economic operations, measures the efficiency with its economy functions, and affords a periodic inventory, that is, an indication of the economic position of a country. These three functions correspond to those of business accounting, the chief difference being that business accounting is conducted exclusively on one level set by the legal structure of the locals.

Social accounting, on the other hand, must be calculated on two levels: first, the combination of existing accounts in accordance with prevailing business methods, and second, the combination in recasting of these accounts to conform with a set of standard rules derived from economic theory. The two levels are designated as "national business accounting" and "national economic accounting." They coexist at any given time.[7]

The interest of accountants and accounting researchers in the field of social accounting in general and national income accounting in particular has, however, declined over the years and was left to economists and social statisticians. Any resurgence of interest in socio-economic accounting would definitely spur more involvement by accountants and accounting researchers in the field of social accounting. In fact, the renewed interest in social measurement in the mid-1960s has spurred research for the development of "social indicators," "social accounting," "measuring the quality of life," "monitoring social change," and "social reporting."[8]

The recent interest of accountants and accounting researchers in expanding the scope of accounting beyond the business enterprise established the area of socio-economic accounting as a full-fledged discipline of interest to accountants and all other social sciences. Various definitions of socio-economic accounting were offered in the literature. Let's examine some of these definitions before proposing a definition befitting the paradigmatic theme of this book. David F. Linowes proposes the following definitions:

> Socio-economic accounting is intended here to mean the application of accounting in the field of the social sciences. These include sociology, political science and economics.[9]

> As I see it, socio-economic accounting is the measurement and analysis of the social and economic consequences of government and business actions on the public sector.[10]

In 1970 Sybil Mobley offered a definition that gives the broadest scope to socio-economic accounting:

> [Socio-economic accounting] refers to the ordering, measuring, and analysis of the social and economic consequences of governmental and entrepreneurial behavior. So defined, socio-economic accounting is seen as encompassing and extending present accounting. Traditional accounting has limited its concern to selected economic consequences—whether in the financial, managerial, or national income areas. Socio-economic accounting expands each of these areas to include the social consequences as well as economic effects which are not presently considered.[11]

Steven C. Dilley rightfully observed that Mobley's definition is broad enough to include any extension of accountants' responsibilities and proposed instead to categorize the various types of social economic accounting into five general areas as follows:

1. National social income accounting
2. Social auditing
3. Financial/managerial social accounting for nonprofit entities
4. Financial social accounting
5. Managerial social accounting.[12]

Each of the above-cited definitions offers one or several aspects of the nature of socio-economic accounting. Put together, they provide a more exhaustive definition of socio-economic accounting as follows:

> Socio-economic accounting results from the application of accounting in the social sciences; it refers to the ordering, measuring, analysis, and disclosure of the social and economic consequences of governmental and entrepreneurial behavior. It includes these activities at the macro and micro level. At the micro level, its purpose is the measurement and reporting of the impact of organizational behavior of firms on their environment. At the macro level, its purpose is the measurement and disclosure of the economic and social performance of the nation. At the micro level socio-economic accounting includes, therefore, financial and managerial social accounting and reporting and social auditing. At the macro level socio-economic accounting includes, therefore, social measurement, social accounting and reporting, and the role of accounting in economic development.

The expansion of the scope of accounting to cover the goals of socio-economic accounting may be rationalized and motivated by some of the new paradigmatic thoughts in the social sciences, namely, the commitment to social welfare, the new environmental paradigm in sociology, the ecosystem perspective, and the sociologizing mode. The avenues for socio-economic accounting include the need for an economic, an ethical, and a rectification paradigm, the need for a micro and macro social accounting, and, finally, the need for social auditing.

### The Economic Paradigm for Socio-Economic Accounting

Corporation-society relationships are governed by the economic principles espoused by the government and the nation. These same principles determine the role of the corporation in society and define the nature of its activities. The continuum of economic principles goes from the extreme right of libertarianism to the extreme left of radical economics. In between these views fall the institutional and social economists.

Both libertarianism and radical economics center on extreme views concerning the preeminence of either the market or the state and present rigid solutions to complex economic and social problems. The social and institutional economists present a more reasoned approach to corporation-society relationships. The social economists may be identified by their deep commitment to human welfare and social justice. The institutionalists may be identified by their commitment to pragmatism and reliance on empirical observation and inductive logic as a way of analyzing economic and social problems. Both the social economist and the institutionalist worlds are the social level of generalization to analyze social organization and process and avoid the atomistic analytical units used by conventional micro-economics.

The interest in human and social welfare in social economics and the interest in a pragmatic approach to problems by the institutionalist may be strengthened by a synthesis of their approaches. Such a synthesis would serve to improve corporation-society relationships in a manner beneficial to both.

> The economic paradigm governing the relationships of corporation and society need not be the role or importance of the market and/ or the state as in libertarianism or the radical economics but a clear statement of national and social justice and experimentation with institutional arrangements to solve economic and social problems.

This synthesis of social and institutional economics is at the heart and within the spirit of socio-economic accounting. It calls for every organizational unit, including the government, to define goals compatible with human welfare and social justice and to look for institutional arrangements suitable to their realization.

### The Rectification Paradigm for Socio-Economic Accounting

We live at a time when there are increasing tensions about the nature of the social contract and the inadequate provision of public goods, economic inequality, and social injustice. Because the corporation is an active market and social agent, its activities can either worsen or correct some of these problems. Thus, the corporation's relationships with society are by definition affected by its role in dealing with the sources of those tensions. The options open to the corporation are on a continuum from complete indifference to an active role in rectifying some of these social problems. Complete indifference would definitely be harmful to the long-term interests of the firm. Involvement in some forms of rectification is a way of ensuring mutual acceptance by society and taking a role in securing social order and affluence.

Socio-economic accounting is by definition compatible with a rectification paradigm. It even implies that rectification is necessary to reassess and improve a business's social conduct. A rectification paradigm motivates and/or explains the corporation's role in reducing social tensions and creating an atmosphere more favorable to and supportive of a business's social involvement in general and socio-economic accounting in particular.

### The Ethical Paradigm for Socio-Economic Accounting

The activities of business corporations have a tremendous effect on their environment in terms of both social costs and social benefits. Indeed, not only is a business corporation first a corporate citizen, but it should be a good corporate citizen. This view of the world presents the business executive with a new set of choices. There are generally two opposite views on the role of management. One, the strict constructionism school, criticizes the social responsibility advocates and argues mainly that profit maximization is the only acceptable objective of business corporations. The other, the social responsibility school, argues that businessmen should be involved in correcting some of the social ills of society. Both views have generated a debate in the corporate-society literature.

Socio-economic accounting is by definition more favorable to the social responsibility school. It even implies ethical guidelines to reassess and improve a business's school conduct. It argues for an ethical paradigm of the corporate-society relationship more favorable to and supportive of a business's school involvement in general and socio-economic accounting in particular.

### An Economic Remedy to Social Issues

For the market to produce an efficient level of output, the private marginal benefit must equal the social marginal benefit and the private marginal cost must equal the social marginal cost. With respect to both conditions, sources of market failure such as imperfect information, consumer ignorance, external economies and diseconomies, and monopoly render the market allocation unlikely to result in an efficient level of output. Similarly, the market fails to provide an equitable distribution of the level of output given the presence of poverty, inequality, and discrimination.

The failure of the market to provide an efficient and equitable level of output for most of the social issues requires some form of government intervention either by directly providing the good or service, by regulating the market, and/or by imposing a system of taxation/ subsidization.

Government intervention has not necessarily met the criteria of efficiency and/or equity in most of the social issues. Experimentation may be needed to find the type of economic organizations most adequate to deal with each of the social issues. For example, the voucher programs in education and in housing, the negative income tax proposals for inequality, and the health maintenance organizations (HMOs) in health care are indicative of the type of experiments needed. *The controversy of market versus nonmarket solutions seems to obscure the real issue, which is to correct some of the social and unfair ills of society.* Experimentation in various forms of economic organizations coupled with the measurement and audit of their social costs and benefits is the key. Socioeconomic accounting, with its emphasis on measurement and audit of costs and benefits, may help choose the type of economic organization needed to deal with each of the social issues.

## Social Accounting

The previous calls for a synthesis of social and institutional economics, a rectification paradigm, an ethical paradigm, and an economic remedy to social issues may only be implemented by an effort at the micro and macro levels to identify, measure, and disclose the total performance, economic and social, of all the economic and social units of a nation. Such is the objective of micro and macro social accounting. Micro social accounting deals with the measurement and disclosure of the social performance of micro-economic units, while macro social accounting deals with the same tasks for the macro-economic units. Micro and macro social accounting constitute an expansion of social accounting to deal with the effects of organizational behavior on the total environment. To accomplish these objectives, theories and techniques of social accounting need to be constructed, verified, and used by micro and macro economic and social units.


### Social Auditing

Public demand for socially oriented programs of one kind or another and for measurement and disclosure of the environment effects of organizational behavior will create pressure for a form of social auditing of the activities of corporations. Given the novelty of the phenomenon and the lack of generally accepted procedures, social auditing tends at present to take forms to accommodate the various views about the ways firms should respond to their social environment. However, as the need for social measurement and reporting increases with a greater acceptance of socio-economic accounting, social auditing may become as standard and as rigorous as financial auditing. The professional "social auditor" will be involved in the social audit and be asked to examine the validity of the social data prepared by the firm.

Socio-economic accounting relies heavily on social auditing for an appraisal of the total performance of profit and not-for-profit entities. These types of audits include social process/program management audit, macro-micro social indicator audit, social performance audit, social balance sheet and income statement, energy accounting and auditing, comprehensive auditing, environmental auditing, human resource accounting, and constituency group attitudes audit.


## ORGANIZATIONAL EFFECTIVENESS AS A CONCEPT OF CORPORATE REPUTATION

The concept of organizational effectiveness or concept reputation focuses on criteria that define organizational success and organizational performance. It is a very difficult concept to define because it connotes a subjective level of overall organizational goodness, and defining that goodness is a highly individual matter.

Researchers have used various methods to operationalize and measure the organizational effectiveness construct. Both univariate and multivariate models have been used. The univariate models of organizational effectiveness searched for a measurement of the attainment of some "ultimate criterion." A review of various univariate effectiveness measures used in the literature identified the following thirty different variables:

1. Overall effectiveness, measured by overall ratings or judgments from knowledgeable persons.

2. Productivity, measured as the quantity or volume of output at the individual, group, or total organizational level.

3. Efficiency, measured as an input or output ratio.

4. Profit or rate of return on assets.

5. Quality of the primary service or product provided.

6. Accidents that result in lost time.

7. Growth, measured as an increase in an important organizational factor such as assets, sales, and so forth.

8. Absenteeism as measured by the number of absences.

9. Turnover as measured by the number of absences.

10. Job satisfaction.

11. Motivation as an organizational index summed across people.

12. Morale as a group phenomenon involving extra effort, goal communality, commitment, and feelings of belonging.

13. Degree of control used to influence and direct the behavior of organizational members.

14. Conflict/cohesion, defined as a continuum from one extreme where members work well together to the other extreme where members are at each other's throats.

15. Flexibility/adaptation, measured as the ability of an organization to change its standard operating procedures in response to environmental changes.

16. Planning and goal setting, measured as the degree to which the firm engages in goal-setting behavior.

17. Goal consensus, measured as the degree to which all members perceive the same organizational goals.

18. Internalization of organizational goals, measured by the degree of acceptance of the goals.

19. Role and norm congruence, measured by the degree to which members agree on such things as desirable supervisory attitudes, performance expectations, morale, and so forth.

20. Managerial interpersonal skills.

21. Managerial task skills.

22. Information management and communication, measured as the degree to which complete, efficient, and accurate information is disseminated to ensure organizational effectiveness.

23. Readiness, measured by the extent to which an organization can perform a specific task.

24. Utilization of the environment, measured by the efficiency in the use of environment resources.

25. Evaluations by external entities with which the firm interacts, such as suppliers, stockholders, enforcement agencies, and the general public.

26. Stability as measured by the maintenance of structure, function, and resources through time and through periods of stress.

27. Value of human resources as measured by the total value of the members of the organization.

28. Participation and shared influence.

29. Training and development emphasis.

30. Achievement emphasis, measured by the degree to which a firm rewards achievement.[13]

These univariate models have been criticized as being difficult to defend as comprehensive or adequate measures of organizational effectiveness and as representing more an expression of the researchers' value systems.[14]

Unlike univariate models, multivariate models of organizational effectiveness focus on integration relationships between important variables that can affect organizational success. They focus, however, on different evaluation criteria or attributes with particular emphasis on the adaptability/flexibility criterion. Examples of the studies using multivariate models of effectiveness and the criteria utilized include:

1. A study by Georgopolous and Tannenbaum[15] that uses productivity, flexibility, and absence of organizational strain.

2. A study by Etzioni that uses environmental orientation, optimal allocation of resources, and goal realization.[16]

3. A study by Bennis[17] that uses adaptability, sense of identity, and capacity to test reality.

4. A study by Simpson and Gulley[18] that uses goal attainment and adaptation to internal and external pressure.

5. A study by Brager[19] that uses citizen involvement in low-income areas.

6. A study by Blake and Mouton[20] that uses simultaneous achievement of high-production-centered and high-people-centered enterprise.

7. A study by Caplow[21] that uses stability, integration, volunteerism, and achievement.

8. A study by Gruskey[22] that uses baseball-team standing.

9. A study by Katz and Kahn[23] that uses growth, storage, survival, and control over the environment.

10. A study by Lawrence and Lorsch[24] that uses optimal balance of integration and differentiation.

11. A study by Yuchtman and Seashore[25] that uses successful acquisition of scarce and valued resources and control over the environment.

12. A study by Likert[26] that uses the intervening variables of loyalty, conflict, pressure, attitudes, and motivations and the end result variables of volume, cost, quality, and earnings.

13. A study by Friedlander and Pickle[27] that uses profitability, employee satisfaction, and societal value.

14. A study by Price[28] that uses productivity, conformity, morale, adaptiveness, and institutionalization.

15. A study by Bennis[29] that uses adaption, collaboration, revitalization, and integration.

16. A study by Maloney and Weitzel[30] that uses a general business model based on productivity-support utilization, planning, reliability, and initiative and a research-and-development model based on reliability, cooperation, and development.

17. A study by Argyris[31] that uses adaptation to external environment, monitoring of internal environment, and achieving objectives.

18. A study by Schein[32] that uses open communication, flexibility, creativity, and psychological commitment.

19. A study by Mott[33] that uses productivity, flexibility, and adaptability.

20. A study by Bidwell and Kasarda[34] that uses pupil achievement output (reading and mathematical achievement).

21. A study by Duncan[35] that uses goal attainment, integration, and adaptation.

22. A study by Gibson et al.[36] that uses production, efficiency, and satisfaction in the short run, adaptiveness and development in the intermediate run, and survival in the long run.

23. A study by Negandhi and Reimann[37] that uses a behavioral index based on manpower acquisition, employee satisfaction, manpower retention, interpersonal relations, interdepartmental relations, and manpower acquisitions, and an economic index based on growth in sales and net profit.

24. A study by Rumelt[38] that uses growth in net sales, growth in earnings, growth in earnings per share, variability in growth rates, price-earnings ratio, return on investment, return on equity, book equity, invested capital ratio, internal financing ratio, and risk.

25. A study by Webb[39] that uses cohesion, efficiency, adaptability, and support.

26. Two studies by Child[40] that use profitability and growth.

27. A study by Dubin[41] that uses effective utilization of resources and utility of output for public at large.

28. A study by Hall and Clark[42] that uses attainment of operative goals of juvenile courts and their organization set.

29. A study by Weick[43] that uses the organizational characteristics of garrulous, clumsy, haphazard, superstitious, hypocritical, monstrous, octopoid, and wandering.

Although most of these models are normative in the sense of specifying what firms must do to succeed, some are descriptive by just summarizing the characteristics of successful firms. Neither type of model can be characterized as "unrealistic" in the sense of being adaptable to all types of organizations.

Eight problems characterize the measurement of organizational effectiveness proposed in these models, namely, construct validity, criterion stability, time perspective, multiple criteria, precision of measurement, generalizability, theoretical relevance, and level of analysis.[44] All of the above discussion lends credence to the uniformly negative conclusions found in the literature that there is only a rudimentary understanding of what is actually involved in or constitutes the concept of organizational effectiveness[45]; that it is an extremely untidy construct[46]; and that it is not researchable and should remain as a conceptually rather than an empirically relevant construct.[47] This pessimism is not warranted if we view effectiveness from one of three broad perspectives in organizational effectiveness, namely, the organizational goal approach, the systems resource approach, or the multiple-constituency view.

## The Organizational Goal Approach

The organizational goal approach views effectiveness in terms of the degree to which an organization is attaining its goals. The greater the goal attainment of an organization, the greater its organizational effectiveness. "Goal" in this context is synonymous with objective, purpose, mission, aim, and task. The definition of goal is crucial to this approach. The most widely used definition of a goal is "[the] desired state of affairs which the organization attempts to realize."[48]

Distinctions have been made between the "official goals," such as those found in the articles of incorporation, organizational charter, and the like, and the "operative goals," which are those actually controlling the organization.[49] The latter are the most important because they are the goals of "the major decision makers,"[50] the "executive core,"[51] or the "dominant coalition."[52]

Goals can be described in terms of a two-component approach, a prescribed-goal approach and a derived-goal approach. The prescribed-goal approach is characterized by a focus on the formal charter of the organization, or some category of its personnel, as the main source of information regarding organizational goals. The derived-goal approach defines the organizational goals on the basis of some functional theory of the investigator, without relying on either the awareness or the intentions of the members of the organization. Both approaches have been criticized—the prescribed-goal approach for its failure or inability to identify the real organizational goals and the derived-goal approach for its reliance on an external basis for the evaluation of effectiveness.[53]

To correct for the limitations of the prescribed-goal approach, Price suggests that goal identification is possible if the following four guides are followed:

1. The focus of the research should be on the major decision makers in the organization.
2. The focus of the research should be on organizational goals.
3. The focus of the research should be on operative goals.
4. The focus of the research should be on intentions and activities.[54]

There are, however, legitimate concerns with goal approach. First, in the case where goals are multiple, transitional, intangible, or part of a means-end chain, there is a larger probability that goal achievement may be difficult to determine.[55] Second, given the differences in goals among organizations, the products of the goal approach may not be generalizable and comparability may be difficult. A solution may reside in the general measures of organizational effectiveness, where knowledgeable individuals are asked to provide ratings of the degree to which an organization has achieved its goal.

A good example is provided by Georgopolous and Tannenbaum's measurement of patient care, which is adoptable for general use.[56] Note the following argument by Price:

Use of the Georgopolous and Tannenbaum measure in the study of different organizations would produce scores permitting comparison of the degree of effectiveness. Comparison would be possible because of the use of a standardized measure. Averaging scores would permit the comparison between single goal organizations and multiple goal organizations. If a multiple goal organization assigns priorities to its different goals, then the average scores could be weighted.[57]

## The Systems Resource Approach

The systems resource approach views effectiveness in terms of the ability of the organization to exploit its environment by acquiring scarce and valued resources. The more resource input that is derived from the environment, the more effective is the evaluation of the organization. The organization can be evaluated by how well it solves the four essential problems of goal attainment, adaption, integration, and pattern maintenance.[58] As expressed by Yuchtman and Seashore, the organization can also be evaluated at any point in the loop of resource acquisition, transformation, and disposal.[59]

Five advantages are attributed to the system resource approach:

1. The unit of analysis or frame of reference is the organization.
2. A primacy is given to the relations between organizations.
3. The approach is generalizable to different types of organizations.
4. Different measurement techniques could be used to measure the same construct.
5. There are guidelines for the selection of empirical measures of effectiveness.[60]

The systems perspective is concerned with both the functional complementarity of the parts of the organization and the organization's links to its environment. Maintaining this complementarity and these links is essential to the survival of the organization and therefore determines its effectiveness.

Criticisms generally made of the systems resource approach[61] include: (1) while optimization is an important component of effectiveness, it has not been measured; (2) while the need for general measures of effectiveness has been recognized, these measures have not been used; and (3) while the concepts in a frame of reference should be mutually exclusive, in the sense that different concepts should refer to the same phenomena, there are serious violations of this rule of classification in the definition of effectiveness.[62]

## The Multiple-Constituency View of Effectiveness

Both the goal and systems recourse approaches should converge and be consistent since they both relate to organizational performance. A study by Molnar and Rogers examined this issue.[63] Goal approach indicators were matched with system resource measures in examining the convergence and consistency of the two approaches. The correlation between the effectiveness measures and four organizational decision-making variables was used. The results showed some consistency but no convergence between the two approaches.

This is a major drawback of both methods. In addition, both approaches arrive at a single set of evaluation criteria and, accordingly, at a single statement of organizational effectiveness.[64] This is a serious limitation leading to the suggestion by Steers that effectiveness be treated multidimensionally so that we can assess various aspects of an organization.[65] It leads also to the thesis that organizational effectiveness is best measured as a composite of many different effectiveness statements about the organization reflecting the criterion sets of different constituencies.[66] This is what is referred to as the multiple-constituency view of effectiveness. That way, organizational effectiveness will measure the extent to which an organization meets the needs, expectations, and demands of important external constituencies beyond those directly associated with the company's products and markets.

A general and eloquent definition of this approach is provided by Connolly, Conlon, and Deutsch:

> In general, then, we treat effectiveness not as a single statement, but as a set of several (or perhaps many) statements, each reflecting the evaluative criteria applied by the various constituencies involved to a greater or lesser degree with the focal organization. In using the term "constituencies" rather than "participants," we mean to emphasize the possibility that individuals and groups not directly associated with the focal organization may form evaluations of its activities, and may be able to influence the activities of the organization to some extent.[67]

This type of effectiveness is also called the participant satisfaction, ecological model, or external effectiveness domain.[68] The organization is viewed as a set of systems generating different assessments of effectiveness by different constituencies. This view calls for the defeminization of the important constituencies, the effectiveness measure used by each of the constituencies, and the consequences of these assessments.

A good example of the multiple-constituency view is the annual reputational index of corporation disclosed by *Fortune* magazine. Basically *Fortune* polls more than 8,000 executives, outside directors, and financial analysts annually. They are asked to rate the ten largest companies in their own industries on eight key attributes: quality of management; quality of products and services; innovativeness; long-term investment value;

financial soundness; community and environmental responsibility; use of corporate assets; and ability to attract, develop, and keep talented people. This index will be used in this book as the ideal measure of corporate reputation.

## UNDERSTANDING FRAUD IN THE ACCOUNTING ENVIRONMENT

Corporate fraud is a social cost that needs to be eliminated to achieve adequate corporate social awareness. The focus is limited here to accounting fraud. Fraud in the accounting environment is on the increase, causing enormous losses to firms, individuals, and society and creating a moral problem in the workplace.[69–71] it takes place as corporate fraud,[72] fraudulent financial reporting,[73] white-collar crimes,[74] and audit failures.[75]

One important issue is the determination of the causes and the provision of an explanation for the situation. One approach has been to rely on descriptive characteristics of the person or the situation that may lead to fraud in the accounting environment. The result had been a list of "red flag" characteristics to be used in the course of an audit. For example, Elliott and Willingham[76] distinguish between situational pressure red flags, opportunity red flags, and personality red flags. Although these descriptive characteristics may be useful in the detection of potential for fraud in the corporate environment, they do not provide an adequate explanation of what fraud occurs in the accounting environment. The field of criminology offers various theories and models that are very much applicable to fraud in the accounting environment and offer various alternative explanations for the phenomenon. They can also be interpreted into a general framework to be used for identifying those situations most conducive to fraud in the accounting environment.

### The Conflict and the Consensus Approaches

The consensus and the conflict approaches are two major views that hypothesize about law and society.[77] Influenced by anthropological and sociological studies of primitive law, the consensus approach sees laws developing out of public opinion as a reflection of popular will. The conflict approach sees laws as originating in a political context in which influential interest groups pass laws that are beneficial to them.

Using the conflict approach to explain fraud in the accounting environment, it can be argued that accounting interest groups presented a
favorable picture of their problematic situations by insisting that they can
control for fraud and worked to get their view of the situation more
widely recognized. The process led to less stringent regulations enacted
for fraudulent reporting cases and white-collar crime. Basically, it fits
with the notion that the criminal law that emerges after the creation of
the state is designed to protect the interests of those who control the
machinery of the state, including the accounting profession.

The consensus approach refers instead to the widespread consensus
about the community's reaction to accounting fraud and to the legislation
enacted. The consensus approach to accounting fraud may have resulted
from either the ignorance or the general indifference of the general public
to the situation. Another explanation is the idea of differential consensus
related to the support of criminal laws.[78] While serious crimes receive
strong support for vigorous actions, crimes relating to the conduct of
business and professional activities generate an apathetic response.

Using again the conflict model of crime, the origin of the fraudulent
practices in accounting may be linked to a society's political and economic development. As a society's political and economic development
reach higher stages, institutions are created to accommodate new needs
and to check aggressive impulses. In the process these monitoring institutions create a system of inequality and spur the aggressive and inquis-
itive impulses that the consensus model of crime mistakes for part of
human nature. It is the powerful elites rather than the general will that
arise to label the fraudulent practices of accounting as criminal because
these crimes affect these elites as they are related to the possession and
control of property. At the same time, members of the same elite constitute a major component of those participating in the fraudulent practices of accounting. Their motivation to engage in the practices remains
the question. The conflict model of crime would attribute the practices
to a system of inequality that values certain kinds of aggressive behavior.
Basically, those engaging in fraudulent practices in accounting are re-
acting to life conditions of their own social class: acquisitive behavior
of the powerful on one hand and the high-risk property crimes of the
powerless on the other hand. One would conclude that the focus of the
attack on fraud in accounting should be toward societal institutions that
led to the isolation of individuals. It implies reorganization of those institutions to eliminate the illegal possession of rights, privileges, and
position.

### The Ecological Theory

An examination of some of the notorious accounting frauds, white-collar crimes, and audit failures may suggest that some criminal types are attracted to business in general and accounting in particular.[79] Therefore, criminal cases are not indicative of a general phenomenon in the field, but the result of criminal actions of the minority of criminal types that have been attracted to the discipline of accounting. This approach is known as the "lombrosian" view of criminology. But with the lombrosian theory of a physical "criminal type" losing its appeal, the ecological theory appears as a more viable and better alternative to an explanation of the fraud phenomenon in accounting. It adopts the concept of social disorganization as a basis of explanation of corporate fraud. Social disorganization implies the decrease in influence of existing rules of behavior on individual members of the group. Criminal behavior in the accounting field is to be taken as the result of a basic social disorganization. First, the weak social organization of the accounting discipline leads to criminal behavior. Second, with the social control of the discipline waning because of the general public indifference, some accountants are freed from moral sensitivities and are predisposed to corporate fraud, white-collar crime, and audit failure. It is, then, the general public's failure to function effectively as an agency of social control that is the immediate cause of corporate fraud, white-collar crime, fraudulent financial reporting, and audit failure.

### The Cultural Transmission Theory

Unlike the ecological theory, which assumes that criminal behavior is a product of common values incapable of realization because of social disorganization, the cultural transmission theory attempts to identify the mechanisms that relate social structure to criminal behavior. One mechanism is the conception of differential association, which maintains that a person commits a crime because he/she perceives more favorable than unfavorable definitions of law violation. A person learns to become a criminal. As explained by Sutherland:

As part of the process of learning practical business, a young man with idealism and thoughtfulness for others is inducted into the white-collar crime. In many cases, he is ordered by a manager to

do things which he regards as unethical or illegal, while in other
cases he learns from those who have the same rank as his own they
make a success. He learns specific techniques for violating the law,
together with definitions of situations in which those techniques
may be used. Also he develops a general ideology.[80]

This mechanism assumes, then, that delinquents have different values
than nondelinquents. Criminal behavior is the result of values that con-
done crime. Criminals have been socialized to accept these values. They
were transmitted with a culture of crime. Their behavior is an expression
of specific values.[81]

Basically, what is implied is that fraudulent behavior in accounting is
learned; it is learned directly, or by indirect association with those who
practice the illegal behavior. An accountant engages in fraud because of
the intimacy of his or her contact with fraudulent behavior. This is called
the process of "differential association." Sutherland explains as follows:

It is a genetic explanation of both white-collar criminals and lower
class criminality. Those who become white-collar criminals generally start their careers in good neighborhoods and good homes,
graduate from colleges with idealism, and with little selection on
their part, get into particular business situations in which criminality
is practically a folk way. The lower-class criminals generally start
their careers in deteriorated neighborhoods and families, find delinquents at hand from whom they acquire the attitudes toward, and
the techniques of crime through association with delinquents and
through partial segregation from law-abiding people. The essentials
of the process are the same for the two classes of criminals.[82]

## Anomie Theories

Anomie, as introduced by Durkheim,[83] is a state of normlessness or
lack of regulation, a disorderly relation between the individual and social
order, which can explain various forms of deviant behavior. Merton's
formulation of anomie focuses not on the discontinuity in the life experience of an individual, but on the lack of fit between values and norms
that confuse the individual. As an example, in achieving the American
dream a person may find himself in a dilemma between cultural goals
and the means specified to achieve them. The solutions that can be

adopted include conformity, innovation, ritualism, retreatism, and rebellion.[84]

Conformity to the norms and use of legitimate means to attain success do not lead to deviance. Innovation refers to the use of illicit means to attain success and may explain white-collar crime in general and fraudulent accounting and auditing practice in particular. The use of innovation may erase the distinction between what is acceptable business mores and sharp practices beyond the mores. Ritualism refers to the abandoning of the success goal but to a compulsive submission to institutional norms. Retreatism is basically a tacit withdrawed from the race, a way of escaping it all. Finally, rebellion is a revolutionary rejection of the goals of success and the means of reaching it.

These adaptations are the result of the emphasis in our society on economic success and the difficulty of achieving it. Deviant behavior is an expected outcome.

> It is only when a system of cultural values extolls, virtually above all else, certain *common* success goals for the population at large while the social structure rigorously restricts or completely closes access to approved modes of reaching these goals for *a considerable part of the same population*, that deviant behavior ensues on a large scale.[85]

Interestingly enough, Merton goes as far as suggesting that deviation developed among scientists because of the emphasis on originality. Given limited opportunity and short supply, scientists would resort to devices such as reporting data that support one's hypothesis, secrecy, stealing ideas, and fabricating data.

Unlike Durkheim, Merton believes that anomie is a permanent feature of all modern industrial societies. Their emphasis on achievement and the pressures that result lead to deviance. The anomie thesis is further explored in the works of Cohen[86] and Cloward and Ohlin.[87] Cohen[88] attributes the origin of criminal behavior to the impact of ambition across those social positions for which the possibilities of achievement are limited. What results is a nonutilitarian delinquent subculture. Individuals placed in low positions accept societal values of ambition but are unable to realize them because of lack of legitimate opportunities to do so. The resulting delinquent behavior is, however, conditional upon the presence or absence of appropriate illegitimate means.

Corporate fraud, fraudulent reporting practices, white-collar crime, and audit failures are a direct result of anomie in modern societies. Basically, delinquent accountants emerge among those whose status, power, and security of income are relatively low but whose level of aspiration is high, so that they strive to emerge from the bottom even using illegal ways. Anomie results from the discrepancy between the generally accepted values of ambition and achievement and the inability to realize them, and from the availability of appropriate illegitimate means.

## A Framework for Fraud in Accounting

The various theories from the field of criminology offer alternative explanations for corporate fraud, white-collar crime, fraudulent financial reporting, and audit failures. They can be integrated in a framework to be used in identifying most situations conducive to those phenomena (see Exhibit 1.1). Basically, the framework postulates that corporate fraud, white-collar crime, fraudulent financial reporting, and audit failures will occur most often in the following situations:

1. Situations in which accounting and business groups have presented a favorable picture of their problematic situation by insisting that they can control for fraud and worked to get their view of the situation more widely recognized. What may exist is a situation in which the accountants and/or businessmen have stated they are taking private actions to avoid public regulation of the phenomena, when in fact their actions were cosmetic changes or camouflage of serious problems in the profession. There have been many examples of situations in which the accounting profession has argued for private regulation of various problems that affect the profession, the discipline, and standard setting, and has thwarted the actions of legislators who were trying to put a stop to the abuses.[89-92] One has only to recall the failures of various congressional committees investigating the profession to enact to illustrate the point. From a conflict approach, this is clearly a situation in which the interests of those who control the machinery of the state, including the power of the accounting profession, are protected from stringent regulation.

**Exhibit 1.1**
**A Framework for Fraud in Accounting**

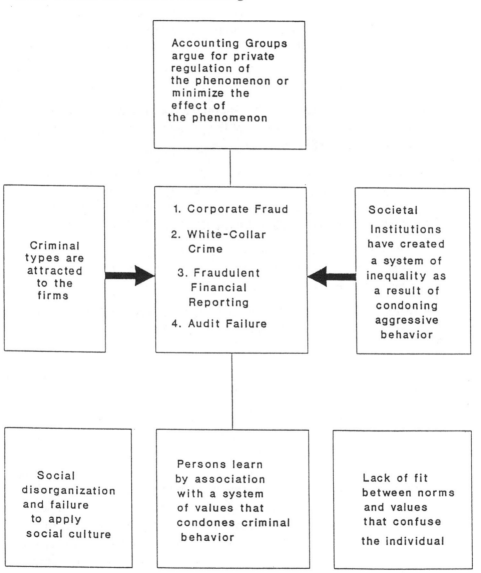

Accounting Groups
argue for private
regulation of
the phenomenon or
minimize the
effect of
the phenomenon

Criminal
types are
attracted
to the
firms

1. Corporate Fraud

2. White-Collar
   Crime

3. Fraudulent
   Financial
   Reporting

4. Audit Failure

Societal
Institutions
have created
a system of
inequality as
a result of
condoning
aggressive
behavior

Social
disorganization
and failure
to apply
social culture

Persons learn
by association
with a system
of values that
condones criminal
behavior

Lack of fit
between norms
and values
that confuse
the individual

2. Situations in which societal institutions have accumulated power, privileges, and position, creating a perception of inequality in those who are not members of these institutions. Basically, the situation may lead to an isolation of individuals in a situation in which the acquisitive behavior of the power is evident in their daily lives. The lower-level accountant may react to this situation of powerlessness, inferiority, and exclusion by resorting to fraudulent practices. It would be a mere reaction to a system of inequality that values aggressive behavior as explained by the conflict model.

3. Situations in which firms in general have attracted some criminal types. This lombrosian view of the phenomena applies to various cases of accounting frauds.

4. Situations in which social disorganization in general and failure to apply social control exist. Basically, weak social organization of the discipline and failure of the general public to be concerned creates a climate conducive to accounting fraud.

5. Situations in which people are placed in a system of values that condones corporate fraud, white-collar crime, fraudulent financial reporting, and audit failures.

6. Situations in which there is a lack of fit between values and norms that confuses the individual.

## CONCLUSIONS

The issues in corporate social awareness center on (a) the adoption of techniques of socio-economic accounting, (b) the maintenance of adequate corporate reputation, and (c) the elimination of fraudulent practices. The implementation of each of these facets of corporate social awareness generates financial outcomes generally beneficial to the firm. Accordingly, the financial outcomes to both the implementation of socio-economic accounting and the maintenance of adequate corporate reputation are examined in the remaining chapters. The end result is that corporation social awareness pays well. It is the right and only game in town for any firm that would like to survive the test of time.

## NOTES

1. Published by Oxford University Press. The American edition was prepared by J. R. Hicks and A. G. Hart and issued under the title *The Social Framework of the American Economy* (New York: Columbia University Press, 1946).

2. Milton Gilbert and Richard Stone, "Recent Developments in National Income and Social Accounting," *Accounting Research* (January 1954), pp. 1–31.

3. John P. Powelson, "Social Accounting," *The Accounting Review* (October 1955), p. 651.

4. Mary E. Murphy, "The Teaching of Social Accounting: A Research Planning Paper," *The Accounting Review* (October 1957), p. 630.

5. Julius Margolis, "The Classification of Sectors in the Social Accounts," *The Accounting Review* (April 1953), pp. 178–186; Carl L. Nelson, "Use of Accounting Data in National Income Estimation," *The Accounting Review* (April 1953), pp. 186–190.

6. E. L. Kohler, "Accounting Concepts and National Income," *The Accounting Review* (January 1952), pp. 50–56; Wilson L. Farman, "National Flow of Funds: An Accounting Analysis," *The Accounting Review* (April 1964), pp. 392–404; Wilson L. Farman, "Some Basic Assumptions Underlying Social Accounting," *The Accounting Review* (January 1951), pp. 33–39; Wilson L. Farman, "Social Accounting in Subsistence and Family-Production Type Economies," *The Accounting Review* (July 1953), pp. 392–400; A. C. Littleton, "Socialized Accounts," *The Accounting Review* (December 1933), pp. 267–271; A. C. Littleton, "Socialized Accounts (II)," *The Accounting Review* (March 1934), pp. 69–74.

7. Mary E. Murphy, "Socialized Accounting," in Morton Backer, ed., *Modern Accounting Theory* (Englewood Cliffs, N.J.: Prentice-Hall, 1966), pp. 466–472.

8. Eleanor Bernert Sheldon and Wilbert E. Moore, "Toward the Measurement of Social Change: Implication for Progress," in Leonard H. Goodman, ed., *Economic Progress and Social Welfare* (New York: Columbia University Press, 1966), pp. 185–212.

9. David F. Linowes, "Socio-Economic Accounting," *The Journal of Accountancy* (November 1968), p. 37.

10. David F. Linowes, "The Accounting Profession and Social Progress," *The Journal of Accountancy* (July 1973), p. 37.

11. Sybil C. Mobley, "The Challenges of Socio-Economic Accounting," *The Accounting Review* (October 1970), p. 762.

12. Steven C. Dilley, "Practical Approaches to Social Accounting," *The CPA Journal* (February 1975), p. 17.

13. John P. Campbell, "On the Nature of Organizational Effectiveness," in Paul A. Goodman and J. Remmings, eds., *New Perspectives in Organizational Effectiveness* (San Francisco: Jossey-Bass, 1979), pp. 36–39.

14. R. M. Steers, "Problems in the Measurement of Organizational Effectiveness," *Administrative Science Quarterly* (December 1975), p. 547.

15. Basil S. Georgopoulos and Arnold S. Tannenbaum, "A Study of Organizational Effectiveness," *American Sociological Review* 22 (1957), pp. 534–540.

16. A. W. Etzioni, "Two Approaches to Organizational Analysis: A Critique and a Suggestion," *Administrative Science Quarterly* 5 (1960), pp. 257–278.

17. Warren G. Bennis, "Toward a 'Truly' Scientific Management: The Concept of Organizational Health," *General Systems Yearbook* 7 (1962), pp. 269–282.

18. R. Simpson and W. H. Gulley, "Goals, Environmental Pressures, and Organizational Characteristics," *American Sociological Review* 27 (1962), pp. 344–351.

19. G. Brager, "Organizing the Unaffiliated in a Low Income Area," *Social Work* 8 (1963), pp. 34–40.

20. Robert R. Blake and Jane S. Mouton, *The Managerial Grid* (Houston: Grief Publishing Co., 1964).

21. Theodore Caplow, *Principles of Organization* (New York: Harcourt Brace Jovanovich, 1964).

22. O. Gruskey, "Managerial Succession and Organizational Effectiveness," *The American Journal of Sociology* 69 (1965), pp. 21–30.

23. Daniel Katz and Robert L. Kahn, *The Social Psychology of Organizations* (New York: Wiley, 1966).

24. Paul R. Lawrence and Jay Lorsch, *Organization and Environment* (Boston: Division of Research, Graduate School of Business Administration, Harvard University, 1967).

25. Ephraim Yuchtman and Stanley E. Seashore, "A System Resource Approach to Organizational Effectiveness," *American Sociological Review* 32 (1967), pp. 337–395.

26. R. Likert, *The Human Organization: Its Management and Value* (New York: McGraw-Hill, 1967).

27. Frank Friedlander and H. Pickle, "Components of Effectiveness in Small Organizations," *Administrative Science Quarterly* 13 (1968), pp. 289–304.

28. James L. Price, *Organizational Effectiveness: An Inventory of Propositions* (Homewood, Ill.: Irwin, 1968).

29. W. G. Bennis, *Organizational Development: Its Nature, Origins, and Prospects* (Reading, Mass.: Addison-Wesley, 1969).

30. Thomas Maloney and William Weitzel, "Managerial Models of Organizational Effectiveness," *Administrative Science Quarterly* 14 (1969), pp. 357–369.

31. A. Argyris, *Intervention Theory and Method* (Reading, Mass.: Addison-Wesley, 1970).

32. Edgar A. Schein, *Organizational Psychology* (Englewood Cliffs, N.J.: Prentice-Hall, 1970).

33. P. Mott, *The Characteristics of Effective Organizations* (New York: Harper & Row, 1972).

34. C. E. Bidwell and J. D. Kasarda, "School District Organization and Student Achievement," *American Sociological Review* 40 (1975), pp. 55–70.

35. Robert B. Duncan, "Multiple Decision-Making Structures in Adapting to Environmental Uncertainty: The Impact on Organizational Effectiveness," *Human Relations* 26 (1973), pp. 273–291.

36. James L. Gibson, John M. Ivancevich, and James H. Donnelly, Jr., *Organizations: Structure, Processes, Behavior* 9 (Dallas: BPI, 1973).

37. A. R. Negandhi and Bernard C. Reimann, "Task Environment, Decentralization and Organizational Effectiveness," *Human Relations* 26 (1973), pp. 203–214.

38. R. P. Rumelt, *Strategy, Structure, and Economic Performance* (Boston: Division of Research, Graduate School of Business Administration, Harvard University, 1974).

39. Ronald J. Webb, "Organizational Effectiveness and the Voluntary Organization," *Academy of Management Journal* 17 (1974), pp. 663–677.

40. John Child, "Managerial and Organizational Factors Associated with Company Performance—Part 1," *Journal of Management Studies* 11 (1974), pp. 175–189; John Child, "Managerial and Organizational Factors Associated with Company Performance—Part 2," *Journal of Management Studies* 12 (1975), pp. 12–27.

41. R. Dubin, "Organizational Effectiveness: Some Dilemmas of Perspective," *Organization and Administrative Sciences* 7 (1976), pp. 7–13.

42. R. H. Hall and J. P. Clark, *Organizational Effectiveness: Some Conceptual, Methodological and Moral Issues* (Working paper, Department of Sociology, University of Minnesota, Minneapolis, 1976).

43. K. E. Weick, "Re-punctuating the Problems," in P. S. Goodman and J. M. Pennings, eds., *New Perspectives in Organizational Effectiveness* (San Francisco: Jossey-Bass, 1977).

44. Steers, "Problems in the Measurement of Organizational Effectiveness," pp. 551–555.

45. Ibid., p. 546.

46. J. P. Campbell, E. A. Bownas, N. G. Peterson, and M. D. Dunnette, *The Measurement of Organizational Effectiveness: A Review of Relevant Research and Opinion* (Minneapolis: Personnel Decisions, 1974).

47. M. T. Hannan and J. Freeman, "The Population Ecology of Organization," *American Journal of Sociology* 82 (1977), pp. 929–964.

48. A. Etzioni, *Modern Organization* (Englewood Cliffs, N.J.: Prentice-Hall, 1965), p. 6.

49. C. Perrow, "The Analysis of Goals in Complex Organizations," *American Sociological Review* 26 (1961), pp. 854–866.

50. J. L. Price, "The Study of Organizational Effectiveness," *The Sociological Quarterly* (Winter 1972), pp. 3–15.

51. M. M. Zald, "Comparative Analysis and Measurement of Organizational Goals," *Sociological Quarterly* 4 (1963), pp. 206–230.

52. J. M. Pemmings and P. S. Goodman, "Toward a Workable Framework," in P. S. Goodman and J. M. Pemmings, eds., *New Perspectives on Organizational Effectiveness* (San Francisco: Jossey-Bass, 1977), pp. 146–184.

53. Yuchtman and Seashore, "A System Resource Approach to Organizational Effectiveness," p. 392.

54. Price, "The Study of Organizational Effectiveness," pp. 5–6.

55. W. Keith Warner, "Problems in Measuring the Goals of Voluntary Associations," *Journal of Adult Education* (Spring 1967), pp. 3–14.

56. Georgopolous and Tannenbaum, "A Study of Organizational Effectiveness," pp. 534–540.

57. Price, "The Study of Organizational Effectiveness," p. 12.

58. T. Parsons, *Structure and Process in Modern Society* (Glencoe, Ill.: Free Press, 1960); F. J. Lyden, "Using Parson's Functional Analysis in the Study of Public Organizations," *Administrative Science Quarterly* 20 (1975), pp. 59–70.

59. Yuchtman and Seashore, "A System Resource Approach to Organizational Effectiveness," pp. 337–395.

60. Ibid.

61. Price, "The Study of Organizational Effectiveness," p. 10.

62. Ibid.; Hans Zeisel, *Say It with Figures* (New York: Harper & Row, 1950), p. 7.

63. J. J. Molnar and D. L. Rogers, "Organizational Effectiveness: An Empirical Comparison of the Goal and System Resource Approach," *The Sociological Quarterly* (Summer 1976), pp. 401–423.

64. T. Connolly, E. J. Conlon, and S. J. Deutsch, "Organizational Effectiveness: A Multiple-Constituency Approach," *Academy of Management Review* 5 (1980), pp. 211–217.

65. Steers, "Problems in the Measurement of Organizational Effectiveness," pp. 546–558.

66. Connolly, Conlon, and Deutsch, "Organizational Effectiveness: A Multiple-Constituency Approach," pp. 211–217.

67. Ibid., p. 213.

68. M. A. Keeley, "Social Justice Approach to Organization Evaluation," *Administrative Science Quarterly* 23 (1978), pp. 279–292; R. H. Kilmann and R. P. Herden, "Towards a Systematic Methodology for Evaluating the Impact

of Intervention on Organizational Effectiveness," *Academy of Management Review* 1, no. 3 (1976), pp. 87–98; R. H. Miles, *Macro-Organizational Behavior* (Glenview, Ill.: Scott, Foresman, 1980).

69. Ahmed Belkaoui, *The Coming Crisis in Accounting* (Westport, Conn.: Quorum Books, 1989).

70. M. M. Levy, "Financial Fraud: Schemes and Indicia," *Journal of Accountancy* (August 1985), p. 79.

71. S. Gaines, "From Balance Sheet to Fraud Beat," *Chicago Tribune*, 28 February 1988, Sect. 7, p. 5.

72. J. Bologna, *Corporate Fraud: The Basics of Prevention and Detection* (Boston: Butterworths, 1984), p. 39.

73. K. A. Merchant, *Fraudulent and Questionable Financial Reporting* (New York: Financial Executives Research Foundation, 1987), p. 12.

74. A. Bequai, *White-Collar Crime: A 20th Century Crisis* (Lexington, Mass.: Lexington Books, 1978), p. 13.

75. K. St. Pierre and J. Anderson, "An Analysis of Audit Failures Based on Documented Legal Cases," *Journal of Accounting, Auditing and Finance* (Spring 1982), pp. 229–247.

76. R. K. Elliott and J. J. Willingham, *Management Fraud: Detection and Deterrence* (New York: Petrocelli Books, 1980).

77. J. T. Carey, *Introduction to Criminology* (Englewood Cliffs, N.J.: Prentice-Hall, 1978), p. 8.

78. D. L. Gibbons, "Crime and Punishment: A Study in Social Attitudes," *Social Forces* (June 1969), pp. 391–397.

79. V. Earle, "Accountants on Trial in a Theater of the Absurd," *Fortune* (May 1972), p. 227.

80. E. Sutherland, "White-Collar Criminality," *American Sociological Review* (February 1940), p. 210.

81. W. B. Miller, "Lower Class Culture as a Generating Milieu of Gang Delinquency," *Journal of Social Issues* 14, no. 3 (1958), pp. 5–19.

82. E. Sutherland, "White-Collar Criminality," *American Sociological Review* (February 1940), p. 212.

83. E. Durkheim, *The Division of Labor of Society*, translated by George Simpson (New York: Free Press, 1964), p. 2.

84. R. K. Merton, "Priorities in Scientific Discovery: A Chapter in the Sociology of Science," *American Sociological Review* (December 1957), pp. 635–659.

85. Ibid., p. 646.

86. A. K. Cohen, *Delinquent Boys: The Culture of the Gang* (New York: Free Press, 1955), pp. 77–82.

87. R. A. Cloward and L. E. Ohlin, *Delinquency and Opportunity* (New York: Free Press, 1955), pp. 77–82.

88. A. K. Cohen, "The Study of Social Disorganization and Deviant Behavior," in Robert K. Merton, Leonard Boorm, and Leonard S. Contrell, Jr., eds., *Sociology Today: Problems and Prospects* (New York: Harper & Bros., 1959).

89. S. H. Collins, "Professional Liability: The Situation Worsens," *Journal of Accountancy* (November 1985), pp. 57, 66.

90. J. E. Connor, "Enhancing Public Confidence in the Accounting Profession," *Journal of Accountancy* (July 1986), p. 83.

91. N. N. Minow, "Accountants' Liability and the Litigations Explosion," *Journal of Accountancy* (September 1984), pp. 72, 80.

92. *Report of the National Commission on Fraudulent Financial Reporting* (Washington, D.C.: National Commission on Fraudulent Financial Reporting, April 1987), p. 2.

## SELECTED READINGS

Akst, D., and L. Berton. "Accountants Who Specialize in Detecting Fraud Find Themselves in Great Demand." *Wall Street Journal*, 26 February 1988, Sect. 2, p. 17.

Belkaoui, Ahmed. *The Coming Crisis in Accounting.* Westport, Conn.: Quorum Books, 1989.

Bell, Daniel. "The Idea of a Social Report." *The Public Interest* (Spring 1969), pp. 78–84.

———. "Social Trends of the 70's." *The Conference Board Record* (June 1970).

Bequai, A. *White-Collar Crime: A 20th Century Crisis.* Lexington, Mass.: Lexington Books, 1978.

Berton, L. "Accounting Firms Can Be Sued in U.S. over Audits Done Abroad, Judge Rules." *Wall Street Journal*, 10 March 1988, p. 2.

Bologna, J. *Corporate Fraud: The Basics of Prevention and Detection.* Boston: Butterworths, 1984.

Buttel, Frederick H. "Environmental Sociology: A New Paradigm?" *The American Sociologist* 13 (November 1978), pp. 252–256.

Campbell, J. P., E. A. Bownas, N. G. Peterson, and M. D. Dunnette. *The Measurement of Organizational Effectiveness: A Review of Relevant Research and Opinion.* Minneapolis: Personnel Decisions, 1974.

Campbell, John P. "On the Nature of Organizational Effectiveness." In Paul A. Goodman and J. Remmings, eds., *New Perspectives in Organizational Effectiveness.* San Francisco: Jossey-Bass, 1979: pp. 36–39.

Carey, J. T. *Introduction to Criminology.* Englewood Cliffs, N.J.: Prentice-Hall, 1978.

Carson, Rachel. *Silent Spring.* Boston: Houghton Mifflin, 1962.

Catton, William R., Jr. "Carrying Capacity, Overshoot and the Quality of Life."
    In J. Milton Yinger and Stephen J. Cutler, eds., *Major Social Issues: A
    Multidisciplinary View*. New York: Free Press, 1978.
Catton, William R., Jr., and Riley E. Dunlap. "Environmental Sociology: A
    New Paradigm." *The American Sociologist* 13 (February 1978), pp. 50–
    53.
Clauson, A. W. "Toward an Arithmetic of Quality." *The Conference Board
    Record* (May 1971), pp. 9–13.
Cloward, R. A., and L. E. Ohlin. *Delinquency and Opportunity*. New York: Free
    Press, 1955.
Cohen, A. K. *Delinquent Boys: The Culture of the Gang*. New York: Free Press,
    1955.
———. "The Study of Social Disorganization and Deviant Behavior." In Rob-
    ert K. Merton, Leonard Boorm, and Leonard S. Contrell, Jr., eds., *So-
    ciology Today: Problems and Prospects*. New York: Harper & Bros.,
    1959.
Collins, S. H. "Professional Liability: The Situation Worsens." *Journal of Ac-
    countancy* (November 1985), pp. 57, 66.
Commoner, Barry. *The Closing Circle*. New York: Knopf, 1971.
Connolly, T., E. J. Conlon, and S. J. Deutsch. "Organizational Effectiveness: A
    Multiple-Constituency Approach." *Academy of Management Review* 5
    (1980), pp. 211–217.
Connor, J. E. "Enhancing Public Confidence in the Accounting Profession."
    *Journal of Accountancy* (July 1986), p. 83.
Daly, Herman E., ed. *Toward a Steady State Economy*. San Francisco: Freeman,
    1973.
Dilley, Steven C. "Practical Approaches to Social Accounting." *The CPA Jour-
    nal* (February 1975), pp. 17–21.
Dunlap, Riley E. "Paradigms, Theories and the Primacy of the HEP-NEW Di-
    mension." *The American Sociologist* 13 (November 1978), pp. 256–259.
Dunlap, Riley E., and William R. Catton, Jr. "Environmental Sociology: A
    Framework for Analysis." In T. O'Riordan and R. C. d'Arge, eds., *Prog-
    ress in Resource Management and Environmental Planning*, Vol. 1.
    Chichester, England: Wiley, 1979.
Durkheim, E. *The Division of Labor of Society*, translated by George Simpson.
    New York: Free Press, 1964.
Earle, V. "Accountants on Trial in a Theater of the Absurd." *Fortune* (May
    1972), p. 227.
Ehrlich, Paul R., and Anne H. Ehrlich. *Population, Resources, Environment*.
    San Francisco: Freeman, 1970.
Elliott, R. K., and J. J. Willingham. *Management Fraud: Detection and Deter-
    rence*. New York: Petrocelli Books, 1980.
Etzioni, A. *Modern Organization*. Englewood Cliffs, N.J.: Prentice-Hall, 1965.

Fairfax, Sally. "A Disaster in the Environmental Movement." *Science* (February 1978), pp. 741–748.

Farman, Wilson L. "National Flow of Funds: An Accounting Analysis." *The Accounting Review* (April 1964), pp. 392–404.

———. "Some Basic Assumptions Underlying Social Accounting." *The Accounting Review* (January 1951), pp. 33–39.

Finterbusch, Kurt. *Understanding Social Impacts:Assessing the Effects of Public Projects.* Beverly Hills, Calif.: Sage, 1980.

Finterbusch, Kurt, and C. P. Wolf, eds. *Methodology for Social Impact Assessment.* Stroudsburg, Pa.: Dowden, Hutchinson and Ross, 1977).

Frendennburg, William R., and Kenneth M. Keating. "Increasing the Impact of Sociology on Social Impact Assessment: Toward Ending the Inattention." *The American Sociologist* (May 1982), pp. 71–80.

Friedlander, Walter A., and Robert Z. Apte. *Introduction to Social Welfare.* Englewood Cliffs, N.J.: Prentice-Hall, 1974.

Friesema, H. Paul, and Paul J. Culhane. "Social Impacts, Politics, and the Environmental Impact Statement Process." *Natural Resources Journal* (April 1976), pp. 339–356.

Gaines, S. "From Balance Sheet to Fraud Beat." *Chicago Tribune*, 28 February 1988, Sect. 7, p. 5.

Georgopoulos, Basil S., and Arnold S. Tannenbaum. "A Study of Organizational Effectiveness." *American Sociological Review* 22 (1957), pp. 534–540.

Gibbons, D. L. "Crime and Punishment: A Study in Social Attitudes." *Social Forces* (June 1969), pp. 391–397.

Gilbert, Milton, and Richard Stone. "Recent Developments in National Income and Social Accounting." *Accounting Research* (January 1954), pp. 1–31.

Hannan, M. T., and J. Freeman. "The Population Ecology of Organizations." *American Journal of Sociology* 82 (1977), pp. 929–964.

Hardesty, Donald L. *Ecological Anthropology.* New York: Wiley, 1977.

Hardin, Garrett. "The Tragedy of Commons." *Science* 162 (1968), pp. 1243–1248.

Katz, Daniel, and Robert L. Kahn. "The Concept of Organizational Effectiveness." In Jainsuigh Ghorpade, ed., *Assessment of Organizational Effectiveness: Issues/Analysis/Readings.* Pacific Palisades, Calif.: Goodyear Publishing Company, 1971, pp. 54–73.

Keeley, M. A. "Social Justice Approach to Organization Evaluation." *Administrative Science Quarterly* 23 (1978), pp. 279–292.

Kilmann, R. H., and R. P. Herden. "Towards a Systematic Methodology for Evaluating the Impact of Intervention on Organizational Effectiveness." *Academy Management Review* 1, no. 3 (1976), pp. 87–98.

Kohler, E. L. "Accounting Concepts and National Income." *The Accounting Review* (January 1952), pp. 50–56.

Levy, M. M. "Financial Fraud: Schemes and Indicia." *Journal of Accountancy* (August 1985), p. 79.

Linowes, David F. "The Accounting Profession and Social Progress." *The Journal of Accountancy* (July 1973), pp. 32–40.

———. "Socialized Accounts (II)." *The Accounting Review* (March 1934), pp. 69–74.

———. "Socio-Economic Accounting." *The Journal of Accountancy* (November 1968), pp. 37–42.

Littleton, A. C. "Socialized Accounts." *The Accounting Review* (December 1933), pp. 267–271.

Lyden, F. J. "Using Parson's Functional Analysis in the Study of Public Organizations." *Administrative Science Quarterly* 20 (1975), pp. 59–70.

McEvoy, James, III, and Thomas Dietz, eds. *Handbook for Environmental Planning: The Social Consequences of Environmental Change.* New York: Wiley, 1977.

Margolis, Julius. "The Classification of Sectors in the Social Accounts." *The Accounting Review* (April 1953), pp. 178–186.

Meadows, D. H., et al. *Limits to Growth.* New York: Universe Books, 1972.

Merchant, K. A. *Fraudulent and Questionable Financial Reporting.* New York: Financial Executives Research Foundation, 1987.

Merton, R. K. "Priorities in Scientific Discovery: A Chapter in the Sociology of Science." *American Sociological Review* (December 1957), pp. 635–659.

———. "Social Structure and Anomie." *American Sociological Review* (October 1938), pp. 672–682.

———. *Social Theory and Social Structure.* New York: Free Press, 1957.

Michelson, William. *Man and His Urban Environment: A Sociological Approach.* Reading, Mass.: Addison-Wesley, 1976.

Miles, R. H. *Macro-Organizational Behavior.* Glenview, Ill.: Scott, Foresman, 1980.

Miller, W. B. "Lower Class Culture as a Generating Milieu of Gang Delinquency." *Journal of Social Issues* 14, no. 3 (1958), pp. 5–19.

Minow, N. N. "Accountants' Liability and the Litigation Explosion." *Journal of Accountancy* (September 1984), pp. 72, 80.

Mobley, Sybil C. "The Challenges of Socio-Economic Accounting." *The Accounting Review* (October 1970), pp. 762–768.

Mohr, L. B. "The Concept of Organizational Goal." *The American Political Science Review* 67 (1973), pp. 470–541.

Molnar, J. J., and D. L. Rogers. "Organizational Effectiveness: An Empirical Comparison of the Goal and System Resource Approach." *The Sociological Quarterly* (Summer 1976), pp. 401–423.

Murphy, Mary E. "Socialized Accounting." In Morton Backer, ed., *Modern Accounting Theory.* Englewood Cliffs, N.J.: Prentice-Hall, 1966: pp. 466–510.

————. "The Teaching of Social Accounting: A Research Planning Paper." *The Accounting Review* (October 1957), pp. 630–645.

Neidinger, Errol, and Allan Schnaiberg. "Social Impact Assessment as Evaluation Research: Claimants and Claims." *Evaluation Review* 4 (1980), pp. 507–535.

Nelson, Carl L. "Use of Accounting Data in National Income Estimation." *The Accounting Review* (April 1953), pp. 186–190.

Ophuls, William. *Ecology and the Politics of Scarcity.* San Francisco: Freeman, 1977.

Parsons, T. *Structure and Process in Modern Society.* Glencoe, Ill.: Free Press, 1960.

Perrow, C. "The Analysis of Goals in Complex Organizations." *American Sociological Review* 26 (1961), pp. 854–866.

Powelson, John P. "Social Accounting." *The Accounting Review* (October 1955), pp. 651–659.

Price, J. L. "The Study of Organizational Effectiveness." *The Sociological Quarterly* (Winter 1972), pp. 3–15.

*Report of the National Commission on Fraudulent Financial Reporting.* Washington, D.C.: National Commission on Fraudulent Financial Reporting, April 1987.

St. Pierre, K., and J. Anderson. "An Analysis of Audit Failures Based on Documented Legal Cases." *Journal of Accounting, Auditing and Finance* (Spring 1982), pp. 229–247.

Seashore, Stanley E., and Ephraim Yuchtman. "Factorial Analysis of Organizational Performance." *Administrative Science Quarterly* 12 (1967), pp. 337–395.

Steers, Richard M. "Problems in the Measurement of Organizational Effectiveness." *Administrative Science Quarterly* (December 1975), pp. 546–558.

Stretton, Hugh. *Capitalism, Socialism and the Environment.* Cambridge: Cambridge University Press, 1976.

Sutherland, E. *White-Collar Crime.* New York: Dryden Press, 1949.

————. "White-Collar Criminality." *American Sociological Review* (February 1940), pp. 210–231.

U.S. Department of Health, Education and Welfare. *Toward a Social Rest.* Ann Arbor: University of Michigan Press, 1970.

Warner, W. Keith. "Problems in Measuring the Goals of Unitary Association." *Journal of Adult Education* (Spring 1967), pp. 3–14.

Wilden, Anthony. "Ecology and Ideology." In Ahamed Idris-Solven, Elizabeth Idris-Solven, and Mary K. Vaughan, eds., *The World as a Company Town.* The Hague: Mouton, 1978.

————. *Ecology and Ideology: The Structure of Domination in Western Society.* London: Tavistock, 1973.

Wilensky, Harold L., and Charles N. Lebeaux. *Industrial Society and Social Welfare*. New York: Free Press, 1965.

Wilke, Arthur S., and Harvey R. Cain. "Social Impact Assessment under N.E.P.A.: The State of the Field." *Western Sociological Review* 8 (1977), pp. 105–108.

Wolf, Charles P. "Getting Social Impact Assessment into the Policy Arena." *Environmental Impact Assessment Review* (March 1980), pp. 27–36.

Yuchtman, Ephraim, and Stanley E. Seashore. "A System Resource Approach to Organizational Effectiveness." *American Sociological Review* 32 (1967), pp. 337–395.

Zald, M. M. "Comparative Analysis and Measurement of Organizational Goals." *Sociological Quarterly* 4 (1963), pp. 206–230.

Zeisel, Hans. *Say It with Figures*. New York: Harper & Row, 1950.

# 2

## The Concept of Social Cost in Socio-Economic Accounting

### INTRODUCTION

Most economists agree that perfect competition in all markets will lead to a position of maximum social welfare, given the assumptions that underlie the analysis.[1] If markets are highly competitive and consumers and procedures are rationally attempting to reach a maximum level of satisfaction, then the available resources will be allocated in a way that maximizes social welfare. In such economic situations:

(a) Procedures will value the marginal product of a variable productive service as equal to its marginal product multiplied by the market price of the commodity in question. Hence, in the case of labor, a profit-maximizing firm would hire additional laborers until the wage paid to the last worker employed just equals the dollar value of the extra product he produces. As Ferguson states: "The individual demand curve for a single variable productive service is given by the value of the marginal product curve of the productive service in question."[2]

(b) Consumers who wish to maximize satisfaction subject to a limited money income will allocate their expenditures so that the last dollar spent on any particular item will yield an amount of satisfaction equal to the last dollar spent on any other item. In other words: "The point of consumer equilibrium of the maximization of satisfaction subject to a limited money income is defined by the condition that the marginal rate of substitution of $X$ for $Y$ equals the ratio of the price of $X$ to the price of $Y$."[3]

(c) If, in addition, the purchasing power distribution conforms to the ethical standards of the society and if consumer control over resource allocation is accepted as ethically correct, then the prices of goods and factors of production represent their accurate contributions to social welfare. As Ferguson states: "If the political organization of a society is such as to accord paramount importance to its individual members, social welfare, or the economic well-being of the society, will be maximized if every consumer, every firm, every industry, and every input market is perfectly competitive."[4]

Thus prices provide automatic, socially valid guidelines for investment and production. But in the case where an obstruction to the private market process exists, then the marginal social cost will not equate with the marginal social benefit and maximum social welfare will not be achieved. A usual case in production occurs when private costs are shifted to other producers. Indirect effects of such nature have been considered in economics by various labels such as "third-party effects," "spillover effects," and, more clearly, "external economies or diseconomies"; they are the social costs not considered by the private marginal cost-pricing rule. The immediate result is that an apparently efficiently working economy, one in which outputs are quickly adjusted so that prices everywhere tend to equate private marginal cost, may lead the economy very far from the optimal social welfare solution. In short: "Optimal solution[s] by micro economic units will not give rise to social optima; on the contrary, they may and will coincide with a disruption of the nature and social environment."[5]

## EXTERNALITIES: THE NATURE AND DIFFICULTIES OF MANAGEMENT

Social cost is a general term for different cost elements. It is defined as covering "all direct and indirect losses suffered by third persons or the general public as a result of private economic activities."[6] In order to be recognized as a social cost, these direct and indirect losses must have two characteristics:

1. It should be possible to avoid them.
2. They are generated by a productive activity and shifted to the society.

For example, pollution of a lake could be related to the productive activities of the neighboring firms and as such it is man-made and could be avoided through different means. Social costs arise, then, because of the emphasis at the firm level on the minimization of private costs (or the maximization of private income). Therefore, the higher the profit motivation, the greater the probability of social costs generated. Social costs are a function of private costs. For one firm, they are those private costs that are not accounted for or "internalized." In other words: "The distinguishing feature of externalities (social cost) is that they are economic relations that do not or cannot go through the market, thus causing people to receive benefits free and to incur costs or endure discomforts without compensation."[7]

Social cost is a major aspect of the "externality" problem. Economists have tried to ascertain the monetary value of externalities and so to bring them within the scope of economic analysis. To date they have not succeeded in doing so. Among the reasons may be the following:

(a) Some types of external diseconomies, manifestly important ones, do not lend themselves easily to measurement. Also the chain of causation may be very complex. As an example: "Air pollution is not only the result of, and not proportionate to the volume of production and the emissions of residual waste products, they are also governed by the interactions of a whole series of variables which may react upon one another."[8]

(b) Even though measurable, external diseconomies may be so largely dispersed that correct and adequate data may be hard to find.

(c) It is difficult to attribute to a specific sector of the economy the consequences of some external diseconomies that depend for their effect upon complementary economic activities. As Knapp explains, "Environmental and social costs must be looked upon as the outcome of an interaction of several complex systems (economic, physical, meteorological, biological, etc.) in which a plurality of factors interplay through a 'feedback process.' "[9]

(d) Furthermore, external diseconomies and social costs depend for their measurement on the magnitude of the social perception and awareness of the issue. It is "a matter of social evaluation, i.e., the magnitude of the social costs depends upon the importance which organized society attributes to both [the] tangible and the intangible values involved."[10]

(e) Moreover, some of the consequences of externalities are intangibles (Ridker speaks of psychic costs[11]), and as such, "even if the available monetary estimates of social costs were complete, they would have to be considered as fragmentary, because some of the social losses are intangible in character and have to be evaluated in other than monetary terms."[12]

(f) Recently, a distinction has been made between separable and non-separable externalities in an article by Otto A. Davis and A. H. Whinston.[13] In the case of separable externalities, only the total costs are affected, not the marginal (incremental) costs. This would follow, for example, if firm A cuts off the breeze from a neighboring hotel and makes it necessary for the hotel manager to install a central air conditioner; the total cost function of the hotel would be increased by a fixed outlay while its marginal cost would stay constant. In the case of non-separable externalities, the marginal cost is affected. As the authors state: "The difference between the separable and the non-separable cases lies in the facts that externality enters the cost function in a multiplicative manner rather than in a strictly additive way." This distinction between separable and nonseparable externalities adds to the difficulties of measurement and of computations of the appropriate charges to be levied.

(g) The above article mentioned the case of reciprocal externalities[14] and the considerable complexities that occur in the assessment of their values. The reciprocal case happens if firm A imposes an externality that raises the costs for firm B, when firm B carries on a production process that creates another externality that raises the costs for firm A. Reciprocal externalities are likely to lead to a merger when they are nonseparable, because neither firm can reach a maximum profit without dependence on the other.

These difficulties of measurement arise because of the complex nature of externalities. Although these are damages generated either in the process of production of certain goods or in their final use by the public, the private marginal cost-pricing rule does not attach any value to these damages. As a result the social value of a good, i.e., the market value of the good minus the estimated value of the diseconomy, will not only be inferior to its market price, but even negative. When the private marginal cost-pricing rule is changed to a social marginal cost-pricing rule, then a social optimum will be reached through the internalization of externality. Hence, Scitovsky maintains that "it is generally true that one can always enhance economic efficiency by commercializing any non-commercial situation or activity and by internalizing any external economy."[15] Mishan distinguishes between two ways of internalization.[16]

1.  Either the firm reduces output until the social value of a good is raised to reach its marginal cost of production.

2.  Or, we may leave the market price unchanged and instead transform the private marginal cost into social marginal costs by adding to the private marginal cost the value of any externality generated through production or use of the good in question.

## TYPES OF EXTERNALITIES

### Nuisance Externalities

Having stated the nature of the problem, we can now proceed to define the different types of external diseconomies to fully appreciate the difficulties of measurement.[17] Nuisance externalities arise between neighbors. A common agreement usually guarantees certain aspects of life among neighbors such as consideration for each other's comfort. When this tacit agreement is not respected, the harmful effects represent the external diseconomy. The court usually attempts to internalize the externality through different means. Apartment house rules, zoning regulations, building codes, and so forth, are some of the steps taken to minimize the nuisance externalities.

### Capacity Externalities

If the capacity of use of something is reached, an externality is likely to occur. Scitovsky gives the example of the delay caused by the entry of a car onto a freeway that has already reached its capacity.[18]

### Supply Externalities

Capacity externalities are short-run phenomena because capacity can always be expanded in the long run. But where the long run does not bring any solution because of fixed capacity, the externality that could arise is labeled as supply externality. An example would be the fixed supply of mineral resources or the allocation of resources whose total stock of supply is fixed.

### Technological External Diseconomies: Social Costs of Business Enterprises

An external diseconomy is said to exist when marginal social cost is greater than marginal social benefit.[19] It is a technological external diseconomy when it is caused by a physical or technical process. The term "technological external diseconomy" includes such classic examples as water and air pollution and can be better explained by considering each of its words. Diseconomy refers to an uneconomical result in the form of a higher cost to society. External economy means that the social cost is borne by economic decision units independent from the one that caused it. Technological refers to the fact that the social cost is transferred from one unit to another, managerially independent unit by a technical or physical linkage between productive processes.[20] There is then a causal relationship between productive activities and business practices on the one hand and significant external diseconomies on the other. In fact, some of the principles of business enterprises favor the emergence of the social costs of pollution. Concentration is one example: "What is overlooked is that the concentration of industrial production may give rise to external diseconomies which may call for entirely new and disproportionate overhead outlays for which nobody is prepared to pay."[21] The social costs of business enterprises are considered to be mainly the following:[22]

1. The social costs resulting from the impairment of the human factor of production.
2. The costs of air pollution.
3. The social costs of water pollution.
4. The social costs of depletion and destruction of animal resources.
5. The social costs of premature depletion of energy resources.
6. The social costs of soil erosion, soil depletion, and deforestation.
7. The social costs of technological change.
8. The social costs of unemployment and idle resources.

In fact, social costs of business enterprises are not a recent phenomenon; the economic literature and different schools of doctrine have always questioned the validity of the welfare-maximizing, self-regulating market processes. Knapp has surveyed the earlier discussions of social costs under the following headings: (a) the classical economists, (b) the historicists, (c) the socialists, (d) Pigou's economics of welfare, (e) Veblen and his followers, and (f) the theory of monopolistic and oligopolistic competition.[23]

## SOCIAL COST IN THE ECONOMIC LITERATURE

Using these headings, it is interesting to elaborate on the evolution of the idea of social costs in economic literature.

### The Classical Economists: Smith and the Theory of Public Works[24]

It is very difficult to associate the classical economists and mainly Adam Smith with the theory of social cost, yet the invisible hand theory, which implies the reaching of optimal solutions of the economic problem, was dependent on three conditions: (a) that free competition exists, (b) that a system of value based on "moral sentiments" would restrain the competitors, and primarily, (c) that the government would engage in the erection and maintenance of "public institutions" and "public works" to prevent and avoid some social losses that would arise if these works were left to the private market mechanism. Thus, Smith's concept of the "duty of the sovereign" toward the creation of "public works" is one example of the classical economist's theory of social costs.[25]

### The Historicists: To an American New Deal

In the nineteenth century, the historicists, including such authors as Auguste Comte, Gustav, Schnoller, and others, were the first and the strongest to refute the thesis that private-market mechanisms could lead to optimal welfare situations. They were the first to use theoretical and empirical cases to show the disadvantages of perfect competition. Reform through social legislation such as social security, equity in income distribution, and others was strongly advocated by the historicists and influenced the American New Deal.

### The Socialists: The Concept of Surplus Value

Social costs are implied in most of the socialist theories. Marx, Sismondi, Engles, Fourier, and others have looked at the exploitation of labor as being the result of a gap between the price of labor (wages) and the laborers' contribution in terms of value to the total product. This failure of an adequate compensation to the worker is seen as a form of social cost. Another form of social cost, considered by de Sismondi,[26] lies in the introduction of new technologies and new methods of production at the price of extraordinary human costs and capital losses. As Sismondi states, "The immediate effects of machinery [are] to throw some of the workers out of employment, to increase the competition of others and so to lower the wages of all."[27] Robert Owen[28] looked at the competitive structure of the economy as a cause of social cost. Frederick Engels[29] was the first to mention the social costs of air pollution. Charles Fourier saw in modern agriculture the responsibility for "landslides, denuding of mountainsides, and the deterioration of the climate."[30]

## Pigou's Economics of Welfare[31]

Pigou was the first to integrate the study of social costs into the terminology and conceptual system of traditional equilibrium economics. He better expressed the problem through the concept of divergences of social and private costs, and mainly as a result of differences between the "marginal social product" and the "private marginal product." These differences or "disservices" were generated by productive activities and could be resolved through the private-market mechanisms. Pigou saw a role for the government to play in resolving the problem of social costs. Such measures as taxes, prohibition, and social legislation were advocated as able to maximize the "national dividend" and hence social welfare.

## Veblen and His Followers

Veblen and his followers elaborated mainly on social costs generated by technical progress, depressions, and monopolistic practices. Technological innovations are seen as the cause of some social losses resulting from the depreciation of the value of capital already invested and the obsolescence of existing equipment. Veblen considers this rapid obsolescence of capital through technological innovations as the principal cause of depression.[32] He sees in the price system a symbol of parasitism. To him, parasitism means such things as "conspicuous waste," "conspicuous consumption," "depersonalization and alienation." Above all, it implies that men have lost their "instinct of workmanship by giving up their handcraft production and by getting cash value as a reward instead of the old creative satisfaction.''[33]

## The Theory of Monopolistic and Oligopolistic Competition

Both theories show that the case of perfect competition does not fit the usual practical situations. They help in identifying social costs by pinpointing the results of monopolistic competition. These results can be characterized by higher prices for less output and diverted demand to less urgently desired goods with the usual consequences of unused capacity and unemployment.[34] As Knapp states, ''The new theory . . . brings into clear focus the social wastes of market situations in which monopolistic elements are present.''[35]

## J. M. Clark and the Theory of Social Cost

John Maurice Clark was one of the great contributors to the theory of social cost. As early as 1923, he pointed out in his book *Studies in the Economics of Overhead Costs*[36] the major dilemma resulting from the conflict between social and private costs and the necessity of using a ''social cost keeping''[37] in order to make the ''social organism''[38] a reality. One of the causes of the conflict between the private and social costs arises out of the essential nature of business enterprises. Hence the private interest tries to maximize net income above the variable costs of operations and to strike a balance between decreased output and decreased earnings while the social interest is more favorable to a ''cut-throat competition''[39] that will lead to a capacity output at any price. Another cause of the conflict is seen as the generation by the firms of ''social waste''[40] and maladjustments. In this case, Clark advocates an awakening of the ''social responsibility''[41] of private industry and the adoption of a social cost keeping. In his words, ''this involves the devising of a system of social accounting that will work better than our present system of financial accounting.''[42]

In his second work, *Preface to Social Economics*,[43] Clark elaborates on the concept of ''social value'': ''the value to society of these utilities consumed by individuals, or the cost to society of these costs that individuals bear.''[44] He mainly criticizes the classical and neoclassical economic theories for their ''assumption of contentment'' where supply and demand tend to equalize and resources tend to be fully utilized. With regard to this approach he declares that money demands and money expenses are only market phenomena and do not reflect anything of the social wants and social costs of a world "full of unpaid costs and unappropriated services."[45] The solution advocated would be consideration of the net economic value of a given service as including (a) potentially exchangeable by-products in the way of service or damage, valued at the price they would presumably command in exchange, and (b) unmarketables measured by a standard devised from market prices.[46]

This interest in "social organism" creating social values through a "social cost keeping" led Clark to elaborate on the appropriate kind of economic systems compatible with his social ideas. Hence in *Economic Institutions and Human Welfare*,[47] Clark looked at the characteristics of both the "laissez-faire" and collectivist system and ended up rejecting both systems as unfit for a "humane and democratically conceived society."[48] The total laissez-faire system was unfit because it was up to the market to take charge of what should be the community values, and the total collectivism was judged undemocratic because of possible manipulation by the government for its own ends, and reduction of the market concepts to accounting devices. In fact, the major reason for rejection of both systems lies in the idea that the balance between social and private cost should not be fixed but "is conceived as an evolutionary process of creative adaptation, operating in the area intermediate between total laissez faire and total collectivism."[49] That area is the so-called "balance economy" or mixed economy where market forces and socially oriented forces will interact to make the conception of human welfare effective.

The above survey of the literature on social costs is not a complete one.[50] More research has been done by psychologists, sociologists, and others on the impact of modern culture on personal maladjustments such as neuroses, human reactions to racism, and discrimination, which are the social costs of social rather than productive processes. Because of the complexity of the problem, let us concentrate on one type of social cost, the social cost of air pollution.

## NOTES

1. The theoretical proofs underlying this judgment will not be presented with great detail. Several different presentations of the subject are available. For example: William Baumol, *Economic Theory and Operations Research* (New York: Wiley, 1958).

2. C. E. Ferguson, *Microeconomic Theory* (Homewood, Ill.: Richard D. Irwin, 1969), p. 365.

3. Ibid., p. 17.

4. Ibid., p. 446.

5. William K. Knapp, "Environmental Disruption and Social Cost; A Challenge to Economics," *Kylos* (December 1970), p. 844.

6. William K. Knapp, *The Social Costs of Private Enterprises* (Cambridge, Mass.: Harvard University Press, 1950), p. 13.

7. Tibor Scitovsky, *Welfare and Competition* (Homewood, Ill.: Richard D. Irwin, 1971), p. 269.

8. Knapp, "Environmental Disruptions and Social Cost," p. 836.

9. Ibid., p. 834.

10. Knapp, *The Social Costs of Private Enterprises*, p. 21.

11. R. G. Ridker, *Economic Costs of Air Pollution* (New York: Praeger Publishers, 1968).

12. Knapp, *The Social Costs of Private Enterprises*, p. 21.

13. Otto A. Davis and A. H. Whinston, "Externalities, Welfare, and the Theory of Games," *The Journal of Political Economy* (June 1962), p. 120.

14. Ibid.

15. Scitovsky, p. 268.

16. J. Mishan, *The Cost of Economic Growth* (New York: Praeger Publishers, 1967), p. 54.

17. We will consider in this paragraph only "technological external diseconomies" because they are a particularity of the production function and generate a social cost. Other types of externalities called pecuniary externalities as labeled by Scitovsky, op. cit., p. 282, include interdependence among producers through the market mechanism. Their losses are matched by somebody's gains, which means that they are diseconomies that cannot be internalized. A good summary of the subject is found in the following publications: Tibor Scitovsky, "Two Concepts of External Economies," *The Journal of Political Economy* (April 1954), pp. 143–151, and *Welfare and Competition* (Homewood, IL: Irwin, 1971), pp. 282–283.

18. Scitovsky, *Welfare and Competition*, p. 277.

19. Ferguson, p. 461.

20. Allen V. Kneese, *The Economics of Regional Water Quality Management* (Baltimore: Johns Hopkins University Press, 1964), p. 41.

21. Marshall Goldman, ed., *Controlling Pollution: The Economics of a Cleaner America* (Englewood Cliffs, N.J.: Prentice-Hall, 1967), p. 86.

22. Knapp, *The Social Costs of Private Enterprises*, p. 27.

23. Ibid., p. 27.

24. Adam Smith, *The Wealth of Nations* (New York: Modern Library, 1937), p. 681.

25. Smith was always aware of the problems when he published *The Theory of Moral Sentiments* (1759), which elaborates on the moral laws and values of human behavior.

26. Sismonde de Sismondi, *Nouveaux Principes d'Economie Politique*, 2nd ed. (Paris; N.p., 1897), Vol. I, p. 92.

27. Knapp, *The Social Costs of Private Enterprises*, p. 32.

28. Robert Owen, *Report to the Country of Lanark* (Glasgow, 1821), reprinted in *Introduction to Contemporary Civilization in the West* (New York: Columbia University Press, 1946), Vol. II, pp. 407–408.

29. Frederick Engels, *The Condition of the Working Class in England* (London: Macmillan & Co., 1887), p. 64.

30. Knapp, *The Social Costs of Private Enterprises*, p. 35.

31. A. C. Pigou, *The Economics of Welfare*, 4th ed. (London: Macmillan & Co., 1932), p. 134.

32. T. Veblen, *The Theory of Business Enterprise* (New York: Scribner's, 1915).

33. A good summary of Veblen's thoughts is contained in: Bernard Rosenberg, *Veblen* (New York: Thomas Crowell Co., 1963).

34. E. H. Chamberlain, *The Theory of Monopolistic Competition*, 6th ed. (Cambridge: Harvard University Press, 1948).

35. Knapp, *The Social Costs of Private Enterprises*, p. 43.

36. J. M. Clark, *Studies in the Economics of Overhead Costs* (Chicago: University of Chicago Press, 1965).

37. Ibid., p. 403.

38. Ibid., p. 403.

39. Ibid., p. 27.

40. Ibid., p. 485.

41. Ibid., p. 485.

42. Ibid., p. 31.

43. J. M. Clark, *Preface to Social Economics* (New York: Farrar & Rinehart, 1936).

44. Ibid., p. 49.

45. Ibid., p. 45.

46. Ibid., p. 49.

47. J. M. Clark, *Economic Institutions and Human Welfare* (New York: Albert A. Knopf, 1957).

48. Ibid., p. 6.

49. Ibid., p. 6.

50. Knapp, *The Social Costs of Private Enterprises*, p. 43.

# 3

## An Example of Social Cost: Air Pollution

### INTRODUCTION

Air pollution is an example of an external diseconomy; its effects are varied.

1. It causes decrease of property values through progressive destruction and premature deterioration of building materials, metals, paint coatings, merchandise, and so forth.
2. Smoke affects human health.
3. It has an adverse effect on plant and animal life.

By economics of air pollution is meant the measurement of the social cost of pollution and the determination of economic solutions to stop it. Wolozin states: "The economics of air pollution is largely directed to two broad areas, both difficult assignments:

1. Measuring the costs to individuals and society at large of the diffusive despoiling of the atmosphere (and the corresponding benefits of cleaning it up).
2. Determining economic measures to stimulate and/or coerce polluters to eliminate or at least cut down their emissions of destructive gases and particulate matter."[1]

Our purpose here will be to point out the problems facing the two broad areas of interest mentioned by Wolozin.

## STRATEGIES FOR THE MEASUREMENT OF THE SOCIAL COST OF AIR POLLUTION

Air pollution is an "external cost of production and consumption." But there are no market forces that will compel the user to consider the costs he imposes on others; one reason might be the difficulties in estimating fully the social costs of air pollution and the determination of a level of pollution that will be socially acceptable. Wolozin poses the fundamental question: "Can we presume with any confidence to measure the total economic costs of air pollution?"[2] One of the main difficulties is its dimensionality. Air pollution is a multidimensional phenomenon. "Its sources are varied, it affects a multitude of objects and it can produce a wide variety of changes in behavior."[3] Another factor is the relationship between the total costs of pollution and the level of pollution. Linearity is implied in a paper delivered by Kneese.[4] However, nonlinearity is assumed by both Wolozin[5] and Ridker.[6] Wolozin looks first at the relationship between costs of abatement and the level of pollution to justify the nonlinearity between social costs of air pollution and the level of pollution. Exhibit 3.1 shows the relationship between various levels of pollution (measured by some composite indices) and the total cost of control required to reach each level of pollution measured on the horizontal scale.

The rationale behind such curve shaping is that costs of abatement would after a while have to increase more rapidly to reach a lower level of pollution. Following that argument, Wolozin states that it is also possible that social costs due to pollution are nonlinear. "An initial range of minimal damage, than a range of rapid rise in damage costs relative to pollution levels followed by a leveling off, even though this might not be reached except near the point of disaster."[7] Such figures would approximate the curve shown in Exhibit 3.2.

As Exhibit 3.3 shows, cost of control and cost of pollution could be represented as two curves. As the level of pollution rises, costs of pollution (or social costs) will grow larger (nonlinearity). Likewise, costs of control will be higher in order to reach a lower level of pollution.

Exhibit 3.4 shows the sum of the costs of pollution and the costs of control and will lead us to conclude that *the social goal of the firm should*

**Exhibit 3.1**
**Cost of Abatement**

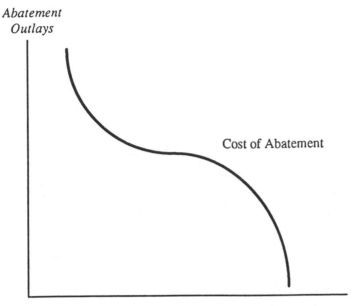

*Abatement*
*Outlays*

Cost of Abatement

*Index of Pollution Level*

*be to reach that level* S *of pollution where it minimizes the cost of pollution and the cost of damages.*[8,9]

Let us assume that Exhibit 3.5 lists the value of the annual total social cost that occurs with no abatement and also the social cost that occurs after different levels of abatement. With 100 percent abatement expenditures, no damages occur. Those estimated are transformed into two curves in Exhibit 3.6, the social cost curve and the abatement cost curve (or the social cost of control). The objective is to select the level of abatement that will minimize both the social cost and the cost of control of pollution. In this example, that point is at 60 percent abatement, as shown in Exhibits 3.5 and 3.6.

Another way of determining the optimal level of abatement for a society is by considering the benefits and costs of abatement.[10] Net benefit will be "the difference between the benefits received by a community from a reduction in pollution and the costs incurred by the community in reducing the level of pollution."[11] It could be expressed by the following equation: $P_i = B_i - SC_i$ where $P_i$ is the total net benefit, $B_i$ the total benefit, and $SC_i$ the total cost of air pollution.[12] *The objective of*

**Exhibit 3.2**
**Social Costs of Pollution**

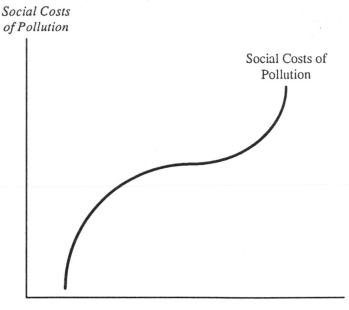

*Index of Pollution Control*

*the technique is to choose that level of pollution that will maximize the net benefits. This was found, in economics, to be where the marginal benefits from pollution are equal to the marginal costs of pollution.*

A benefit from abatement schedules could be obtained for the total social cost of air pollution scheduled in Exhibit 3.5. For example, with no control, the social costs of air pollution are equal to $500. With 10 percent control, they are equal to $380. As a general rule:

$$B_i = TSC_{i=100} - SC_i$$

where

$i = \%$ level of control $0 \leqslant i \leqslant 100$

$SC_i$ = social cost of air pollution with $i$ level of control.

The results are tabulated in Exhibit 3.7 and graphed in Exhibit 3.8 and Exhibit 3.9.

**Exhibit 3.3**
**Cost of Control and Cost of Pollution**

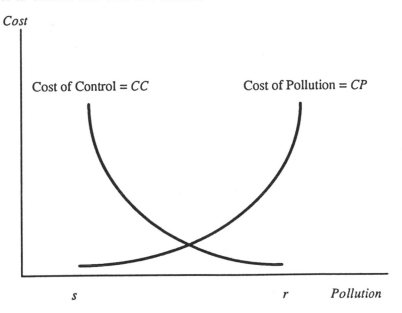

The optimal point of control that maximizes net benefits is the point where marginal benefits are equal and hence intersect marginal cost. This level is at 60 percent.

*At the firm level the manufacturer who wishes to planify an efficient allocation of resources could add as a constraint the above-determined optimum level of pollution, which minimizes net social benefits as an additional constraint.*

Other different methods have been used toward the determination of the optimum level of pollution control that minimizes the total costs of air pollution. An interesting example is the use of cost-effectiveness analysis by W. E. Jackson, H. C. Woblers, and W. Decoursey.[13]

They elaborated a six-step procedure that consists of:

1. Examining present emissions rates by source category to evaluate the existing degree of air pollution controls.

2. Evaluating regional trends to make future projections of controlled and uncontrolled emissions.

3. Evaluating emission control trends that have been established in the region.

**Exhibit 3.4**
**Sum of the *CC* + *CP***

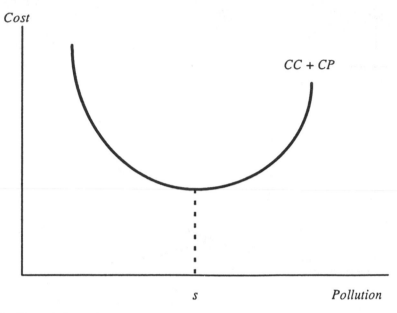

4. Examining alternate control schemes that may be feasible for application to each source category.

5. Determining emission control costs.

6. Using a technique to determine the control scheme with the optimum cost-effectiveness aspect.

Another example has been the use of linear programming and systems analysis.[14-16]

All these models (cost benefit analysis, system analysis, cost-effectiveness analysis, linear programming models) are intended to determine that level of control that allows a minimization of the total social cost of air pollution, but the problem still will be to define strategies for the estimation of the social costs and costs of control of air pollution.

## ESTIMATION OF THE SOCIAL COSTS OF AIR POLLUTION

In order to estimate the social costs of air pollution at a macro or regional level, Ridker[17] developed the following strategy, which I assume

**Exhibit 3.5**
**Social Cost of Air Pollution and Social Cost of Control**

| Level of Control, % | Social Cost of Pollution | Social Cost of Control | Total Cost |
|---|---|---|---|
| 0 | $500 | $0 | $500 |
| 10 | 380 | 10 | 390 |
| 20 | 280 | 20 | 300 |
| 30 | 210 | 30 | 240 |
| 40 | 150 | 50 | 200 |
| 50 | 95 | 80 | 175 |
| 60 | 65 | 100 | 165 |
| 70 | 40 | 250 | 290 |
| 80 | 30 | 300 | 330 |
| 90 | 20 | 450 | 470 |
| 100 | 0 | 500 | 500 |

could be applied at the firm level. He considered a community where ambient air quality is measured on a scale—for example, annual geometric sulfuration rate. If this rate increases, its effects could be divided into three categories.

1. Direct and immediate effects in the absence of adjustments.
2. Individual adjustments.
3. Market effects.

These three categories constitute different levels of analysis of the social costs of air pollution.

### The Direct Effects: The Cost of Air Pollution in the Absence of Adjustments

Ridker assumes that in the absence of individual adjustments and social interactions, the first level of social cost estimate will be computed using three types of information:

1. It is required to determine the damage function per unit of each object affected as a function of the air pollution level.[18] It could be represented by

$$D_i = 2F_i(S), i = (1, \ldots h)$$

**Exhibit 3.6**
***CC + CP* at a Minimum**

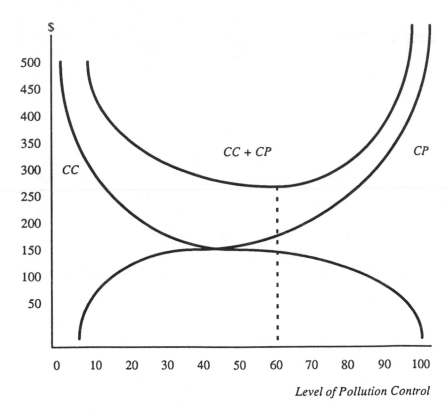

*Level of Pollution Control*

which is a measure of the *i* type of damage per unit of object affected by the pollution and *S* is a measure of pollution.

($SO_2$, for example)

2. A monetary weight of the cost per unit of damage must be obtained.
3. The number of objects affected should be available. Then, if $C_i$ is the cost per unit of damage and $Q_i$ the number of units affected, the social costs of air pollution in the absence of adjustments could be expressed as

$$TC_i = \mathop{E}_{i=1}^{n} [Q_i F_i (S)]$$

**Exhibit 3.7**
**Cost-Benefit Table, Hypothetical Example**

| Level of Control $i$ | Benefit from Control $B_i$ | Cost of Control $Cc_i$ | Net Benefit $P_i$ | Marginal Benefit $Mp_i$ | Marginal Cost of Control $MC_i$ |
|---|---|---|---|---|---|
| 0 | 0 | 0 | 0 | — | — |
| 10 | 120 | 10 | 110 | — | — |
| 20 | 220 | 20 | 200 | 10.0 | 1.0 |
| 30 | 290 | 30 | 260 | 7.0 | 1.0 |
| 40 | 350 | 50 | 300 | 6.0 | 2.0 |
| 50 | 405 | 80 | 325 | 5.5 | 3.0 |
| 60 | 435 | 100 | 335 | 3.0 | 3.0 optimum |
| 70 | 460 | 250 | 210 | 2.5 | 5.0 |
| 80 | 470 | 300 | 170 | 3.0 | 5.0 |
| 90 | 480 | 450 | 30 | 1.0 | 5.0 |
| 100 | 500 | 500 | 0 | 2.0 | 5.0 |

## Individual Adjustments

Ridker refers to possible actions taken by individuals to adjust to the change in environment quality. He gives the following example:

> Consider a person who suddenly finds his asthma getting worse because the level of pollution is increasing. On the most general level, he may do nothing, simply suffering the additional discomfort involved; or he may change his behavior in response to a deteriorating environment. The change in his behavior may be of three different types: First, the individual may change the amount of time he spends in the affected area, for example, by taking longer vacations outside the area of his residence; second . . .[19]

Each of the actions taken by the individual leads to a loss in utility, and the difficulty of measuring its costs is related to the "psychic" character of the possible losses. However, if we do not add the individual adjustments to $TC_i$, the total social costs of air pollution will certainly be understated.

## Market Effects

This starts from the assumption that any adjustment by an individual has an effect on other individuals. "Perhaps the most important inter-

**Exhibit 3.8**
**Determination of Minimum Cost Using Marginal Curves**

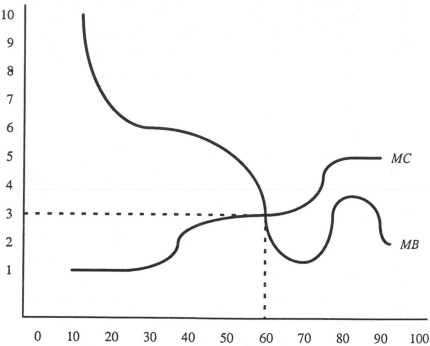

actions for our purpose are the effects that occur because people are linked together by their purchases and sales in different markets.''[20] One example is the increase in the rent in the sector not yet affected by air pollution. Here again there is a measurement problem and Ridker assumes that the only way to measure the market effect is to estimate the change in consumer and producer surpluses and to sum those surpluses over the affected markets. However, he admits the difficulties of doing so and assumes that the total cost of air pollution could better be understated by $TC_i$: the direct effects without individual adjustments.

## DIFFICULTIES OF MEASUREMENT OF SOCIAL COST OF AIR POLLUTION

Besides the individual adjustments and market effects mentioned by Ridker, the difficulties of measurement of the social costs of air pollution are numerous. Let us examine some of them:

First, some of the damages are difficult to measure and the experimental studies used may lack external validity.[21] Haltman, for ex-

**Exhibit 3.9**
**Determination of Minimum Cost Using Marginal Curves**

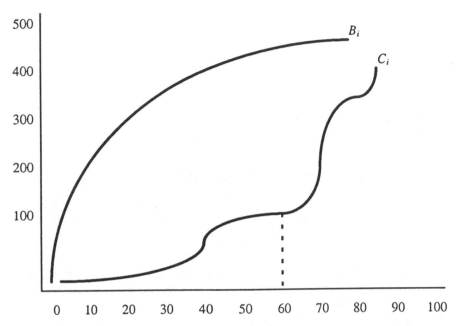

ample, recognizes that it is difficult to establish a quantitative relationship between disease rates and specific pollutant levels.[22] He assumes that the best that can be done is to estimate the average and total costs of these diseases and to suggest roughly the magnitude of the costs that might be the result of air pollution.[23]

Second, useful measurements of economic costs of air pollution must be made "within a specific air shed" and/or specific pollutants.[24] The concept of air shed is vague.

Third, chronic effects of air pollution are usually less considered than acute effects, although it is known that in the long run they may have a harmful effect on human, animal, and plant life.[25] Because they are usually undetected, these chronic costs of air pollution are uncounted and as such there will be an understatement of the total costs of air pollution.

Fourth, air pollution is not the only externality affecting the environment and as such it is difficult to estimate the damages inherent only to air pollution. Externalities are a multidimensional phenomenon with varied sources. Air pollution is an externality and as such "cannot be studied and controlled in isolation, for it is one of a number of inter-related problems affecting the quality of the environment.''[26]

## THE PROBLEM OF CONTROL

We have already stated that the economics of air pollution includes two broad areas, the measurement aspect and the control aspect. The control aspect consists of the elaboration of economic and legislative measures toward the motivation of polluters into controlling air pollution. Let us elaborate on some of these measures.

### Legislation: The Air Quality Act of 1967

The Air Quality Act is one of the measures advocated through legislation, in other words, the outlaw of external diseconomies. In the case of air pollution, the Air Quality Act of 1967 provided a framework for government and industry association toward controlling air pollution. It amended the air act of 1963[27] in the sense that (a) it allowed state control of air pollution problems recognizing herein the existence of differences in controls of different regions, and (b) it enabled the Department of Health, Education, and Welfare to impose standards of air quality if the state fails to do so.

However, the 1967 Air Quality Act has been criticized for different deficiencies.[28]

(a) It emphasizes the adoption of air quality standards (ambient air standards) when it should call for immediate reduction of industrial emissions. ''National industrial emissions standards should precede ambient air standards as a logical and necessary prerequisite to their attainment.''[29] The reason is that air quality standards define a certain limit to pollution rather than identifying the pollutants and providing rules to stop them. As O'Fallon states:[30] ''An ambient air quality standard says in effect that a given pollutant should not exceed a predetermined level in the atmosphere because of aesthetic, economic, or health effects. Emission standards, on the other hand, limit the permissible discharge from sources of pollution.''

(b) The act tries to give to the states the responsibility of enacting a standard to control air pollution. But air pollution is a metropolitan problem and, historically, local authorities took the lead in abating air pollution. This state-oriented approach represents a centralization for problems that are basically different. Air pollution is generated from different cities and as such requires the specific attention of each concerned city. Besides, "it will be difficult for states to bridge the gap of years of experience in this field in order to become full-fledged partners with local and regional agencies."[31]

## The Economist's View: Effluent Fees

A second approach to environmental problems is taxation and mainly effluent fees.[32] As one author states: "Corrective taxes and subsidies are deemed to be required in order to satisfy the necessary conditions for optimality when external effects are observed to be present."[33] This has also been advocated strongly by Croker,[34] Mills,[35] and Vickery.[36] They maintain that the objective of effluent fees would be to place all costs resulting from a specific individual action on the individual who caused it. Under this concept an air polluter would be assessed a tax equal to the damages resulting from his productive activities. This tax amount would then represent the marginal costs he imposed on others. This point of view of "internalizing" the social cost of air pollution through a government-levied charge on the polluters has been praised and criticized. Among the advantages are:

1. A system of efficient fees is flexible. It could be adopted to different situations. For example, fees could increase or decrease depending on the weather conditions, the time of the day, and other factors.

2. Under such a system, management rather than government has to take the decision of accepting the effluent fees or abating pollution. Implicit in the effluent fees' point of view "is recognition that the optimal level of air pollution abatement is closely tied to the technological process involved, with the least cost solution being in many cases a complex combination of process changes and treatment of effluents."[37]

However, some reservations have been raised, particularly the following:

1. A major drawback is seen in the difficulty of measuring and identifying the damages attributable to particular air pollutants, which leads to a degree of skepticism on the efficacity of the

existing technology in effectively enforcing an affluent fee system. The difficulty of inspecting, metering, and monitoring air pollution stems from the fact that the number of small emitters and of emitters difficult to meter is largely contributing to air pollution.[38]

2. Wolozin questions the belief that taxation has an impact on business policies and human behavior: "To support the contention that externalities can be internalized through effluent fees, proponents generally fall back upon a conventional economic analysis of the nature of business behavior in the modern world, a model of business behavior which has been questioned seriously in the literature on the subject and one which very few economists adhere to rigorously in explaining the behavior of the firm or industry."[39]

This contention of the inapplicability of the neoclassical profit maximization model of business behavior to the kind of situations in which effluent fees have to be used is relating to the investment decision in business firms. Proof of the thesis that taxes or effluent fees would lead business management to adopt an abatement program and to authorize inherent outlays is lacking and difficult to validate.

In sum, efficient fees are theoretically founded but practically very difficult to enforce. Air pollution cannot be studied and controlled in isolation. It interferes with other factors that affect the quality of the environment, so an overall approach to directly control externalities could be considered and would allow significant economies.

### Payments

Besides the effluent fee system, alternative approaches exist to control air pollution, such as payments and direct regulation. Direct regulation has been discussed as part of the legislative process and is best expressed by the Air Quality Act of 1967. Payment is an original type of subsidy to restrict waste disposal. It consists of providing payments to a firm for each amount of waste withheld. In other words, this system will be similar in theory to the effluent fee system, but opposite in approach. These payments could take the indirect form of tax credits, investment credit, accelerated depreciation, or a tax write-off of capital cost.[40] The payment system suffers from a major handicap. The concept of paying a polluter is very far from the concept of equitable practice, especially if such payments must be provided through increased personal taxation.

## Methods of Control for the Firm

The three general methods of air pollution abatement are mentioned by the technical progress report of the Los Angeles County Air Pollution Control District.[41]

1. *Installation of control equipment to convert the pollutant gases to a harmless form.* This necessitates a cost analysis of the different steps of introducing such equipment.[42] They are as follows:
   a. Initial cost of equipment
      *1.* Purchase price
      *2.* Freight in
      *3.* Installation
   b. Disruption of normal production during installation
      *1.* Overtime
      *2.* Above-normal scrap materials and labor
      *3.* Time for nonproductive and supervisory personnel
   c. Depreciation policy
      *1.* New equipment
      *2.* Present plant changes
   d. Maintenance
      *1.* Full-time or part-time personnel
      *2.* Possible shutdown periods
      *3.* Supplies, bags, etc.
      *4.* Containers (drums or collecting devices for pollutants)
      *5.* Pollutant removal costs
      *6.* Charges, if any, for dumping (land rental or purchase)
   e. Renovation of present plant
      *1.* Space for collection area
      *2.* Others . . .
2. *Modification of redesign of the basic equipment* so as to minimize or eliminate the problem. An example would be the eventual use of crucible furnaces instead of direct-flame furnaces in melting operations.
3. *Changes in the production process* so as to reduce or eliminate the pollutants. An example would be the substitution of natural gas for sulfur-bearing fuel oil.

Any firm introducing a pollution abatement program would compare the feasibility and cost of using the three alternatives.

## CONCLUSION

An attempt has been made in this brief survey to elaborate on the nature and difficulties of measurement of externalities. As an example, air pollution problems were examined. Here the discussion was focused on the difficulties of measurement and the different approaches to control air pollution. One solution may lie in the involvement of business firms in measuring and controlling the air pollution they generate. In fact, most of the big business firms are committing funds to the control of air pollution[43] and most of these businesses are disclosing their pollution control expenditures in two parts: a verbal description and/or a quantitative reporting part. This current trend toward publicizing dollar expenditures for pollution control leads to a possible broadening of the scope of accounting to include social data and enable the annual reports of business enterprises to become "all-purpose." One proponent of this view states, "Accounting as an organized profession has the responsibility to transcend the internal viewpoint of a private firm and to develop information which portrays a private firm's role in and contribution to society."[44] Opposite views exist in the accounting literature.[45]

With a broader social scope, accounting can and should provide information on pollution costs. However, for the sake of comparability of annual reports, adequate techniques of reporting of these costs ought to be devised.

## NOTES

1. Harold Wolozin, "The Economists of Air Pollution: Central Problems," *Law and Contemporary Problems* 33, no. 2 (Spring 1986), p. 227.

2. Wolozin, p. 288.

3. Ronald G. Ridker, *Economic Costs of Air Pollution, Studies in Measurement* (New York: Frederick A. Praeger Publishers, 1968), p. 13.

4. Allen V. Kneese, "How Much Is Air Pollution Costing Us in the United States?," in *Proceedings: The Third National Conference on Air Pollution* (New York: Public Health Service, Publishers, 1967).

5. Wolozin, p. 229.

6. Ridker, p. 13.

7. Wolozin, p. 229.

8. Ridker, p. 4.

9. Allen V. Kneese, in *The Economics of Regional Water Quality Management* (Baltimore: Johns Hopkins University Press, 1964), p. 4, uses the same analysis to find the level of water quality. The analysis is as follows: "$X$ is the optimum level of water quality in the sense that the costs associated with waste disposal are at a minimum there. These costs include both damage costs and abatement costs. The results indicated above can also be stated in terms of differential calculus. The firm confronts two damage functions, $D_1$ and $D_2$, and a treatment cost $TC$."

The following conditions hold:

$$D_1 = f_1(R) \quad F_2^1(R) < 0$$
$$D_2 = f_2(R) \quad F_2^1(R) < 0$$
$$TC = f_3(R) \quad F_3^1(R) > 0$$

The objective function is to minimize:

$$Z = D_1 + D_2 + TC = f_1(R) + f_2(R) + f_3(R)$$

which will be the case when:

$$\frac{dZ}{dR} = \tfrac{1}{2}(R) + F_2^1(R) + F_3^1(R)$$

if

$$\frac{d^2Z}{dR^2} > 0$$

10. Richard D. Wilson and David W. Minnotte, "A Cost Benefit Approach to Air Pollution Control," *Journal of the Air Pollution Control Association* (May 1969), pp. 303–323.

11. Wilson and Minnotte, p. 304.

12. Wilson and Minnotte considered first only the cost of control of air pollution. Second, because of the existence of $n$ emitters and $m$ receptor areas, the cost of control $CC_T$ was set equal to $\sum_{i=1}^{m} CC_j$ where $CC_j$ is the cost of control for the $j^{th}$ of the $n$ polluting emitters, and $B_T = \sum_{i=1}^{m} \sum_{j=1}^{n} B_{ji}$ where $B_{ji}$ was the benefit received in the $i^{th}$ of $m$ reception areas due the control of the $j^{th}$ of the $n$ emitters. Thus the equation for the net benefits was:

$$P_T = \sum_{i=1}^{m} \sum_{j=1}^{n} B_{ji} - \sum_{j=1}^{n} CC_j$$

13. W. E. Jackson, H. C. Woblers, and W. Decoursey, "Determining Air Pollution Costs," *The Journal of Air Pollution Control Association* (December 1969), pp. 971–982.

14. L. Louch, et al., "Linear Programming Models for Water Pollution Control Programs," *Management Science* (December 1967), pp. 166–181.

15. R. Wilson and A. Bunyard, "A Systematic Procedure for Determining the Cost of Controlling Particulate Emission from Industrial Sources," in *Proceedings of the Air Pollution Control Association* (New York: June 1969).

16. L. Louch, et al., "Linear Programming Models for Water Pollution Control Programs," *Management Science* (December 1967), pp. 166–181.

17. Ridker, p. 14.

18. Ibid., p. 14.

19. Ibid., p. 31.

20. Ibid., p. 21.

21. Arthur C. Stern, ed., *Air Pollution* (New York: Academic Press, 1962).

22. Ridker, p. 30.

23. Ibid., p. 30.

24. Ibid., p. 9.

25. H. Wolozin and B. Landau, "Crop Damage from Sulfur Dioxide," *The Journal of Farm Economics* (October 1966), p. 394.

26. Wolozin, p. 237.

27. J. Martin and F. Syminton, "A Guide to the Air Quality Act of 1967," *Law and Contemporary Problems* 33 (Spring 1968), p. 239.

28. John E. O'Fallon, "Deficiencies in the Air Quality Act of 1967," *Law and Contemporary Problems* 33 (Spring 1968), p. 275.

29. Ibid., p. 277.

30. Ibid., p. 278.

31. Ibid., p. 289.

32. Norman F. Ramsey, "We Need a Pollution Tax," *Bulletin of Atomic Scientists* (April 1970), p. 3.

33. A. Buchanan, *Cost and Choice* (Chicago: Markham Publishing Co., 1969), p. 70.

34. T. Croker, *Some Economic Aspects of Air Pollution Control with Particular Reference to Polk Country, Florida, U.S.* (Public Health Service Grant, AP-00389–02, January 1968), p. 282.

35. J. Mills, "Federal Fiscal Policy in Air Pollution Control," in *Proceedings of the Air Control Association Meeting* (Cleveland: June 11, 1967).

36. A. Vickery, "Theoretical and Practical Possibilities and Limitations of a Market Mechanism Approach to Air Pollution Control," in *Proceedings of the Air Control Association Meeting* (Cleveland: June 11, 1967).

37. George Hagevisk, "Legislating for Air Quality Management: Reducing Theory to Practice," *Law and Contemporary Problems* 33, no. 2 (Spring 1968), p. 369.

38. Ibid., p. 369.

39. Kneese, pp. 192–195.

40. Paul R. McDaniel and Alan S. Kaplinsky, "The Use of the Federal Income Tax System to Combat Air and Water Pollution: A Case Study in Tax Expenditure," *Environmental Affairs* 1, no. 9 (April 1971), pp. 12–32.

41. "Control of Stationary Sources," *Technical Progress Report* (Air Pollution Control District, County of Los Angeles: April 1960), Vol. 1, p. 4.

42. Alvah Bearse, "Air Pollution: A Case Study," *Management Accounting* (September 1971), p. 18.

43. "The Arithmetic of Quality," *Wall Street Journal*, 9 December 1971, p. 71.

44. Floyd A. Beams, and Paul E. Fertig, "Pollution Control through Social Conversion," *Journal of Accounting* (November 1971), p. 37.

45. Hence Professor Paton says: "The notion that the goal of the professional accountant is public or social service is nonsense. His function is to provide the best possible service to his specific clients, the people who pay for his efforts." William A. Paton, "Earmarks of a Profession and the APB," *Journal of Accounting* (January 1971), p. 41.

## SELECTED READINGS

Baumol, William. *Economic Theory*. Homewood, Ill.: Richard D. Irwin, Inc., 1969.

———. *Welfare Economics and the Theory of State*, 2nd ed. Cambridge: Harvard University Press, 1965.

Chamberlain, E. H. *The Theory of Monopolistic Competition*, 6th ed. Cambridge: Harvard University Press, 1968.

Goldman, Marshall. *Controlling Pollution—The Economics of a Cleaner America*. Englewood Cliffs, N.J.: Prentice-Hall, 1967.

Knapp, K. W. *The Social Costs of Private Enterprise*. Cambridge: Harvard University Press, 1950.

Kneese, Allen. *Economics and the Environment*. Washington: Resources for the Future; Baltimore: Johns Hopkins University Press, 1970.

———. *Quality of the Environment—An Economic Approach to Some Problems in Using Land, Water and Air*. Washington: Resources for the Future; Baltimore: Johns Hopkins University Press, 1965).

Ridker, Ronald G. *Economic Costs of Air Pollution, Studies in Measurement*. New York: Frederick A. Praeger Publishers, 1968.

Stern, Arthur C., ed. *Air Pollution*. New York: Academic Press, 1962.

Wolozin, Harold, ed. *The Economics of Air Pollution—A Symposium*. New York: W. W. Norton, 1966.

**4** _____

# Financial Outcomes of Corporate Effectiveness: The Impact on CEO Compensation

## INTRODUCTION[1]

The objective of this chapter is to present evidence on the determinants of executive compensations in the United States. Empirical research on the relationship between executive compensation and firm performance results from the thesis that such relationship is expected if executives act in the interest of shareholders. Several empirical studies of executive compensation tested the relative importance of sales and profit as determinants of executive salaries to determine whether executive compensation encouraged sales maximization or profit maximization, under the assumption advanced by Baumol[2] that profit maximization is preferred by the shareholders. Even after controlling for size, the results are mixed, and where the relationship between compensation and firm performance is significant, the firm performance variables differ.

The main assumption in all these studies is that profit and/or sales are indicators of executive performance. By restricting the examination of independent variables to size and profitability these studies restrict the internal managerial control mechanisms at the disposal of a corporation's compensation-setting board. This restriction results from the traditional neoclassical managerial productivity approach to wage determination where performance is the principal determinant of compensation. Examples of other determinants include (a) the management turnover decision[3] and (b) the personal characteristics of individual executives.[4] Other forces from outside the institution can also bring pressure on the firm's compensation-setting board or committee to reassess the level of executive compensation. The perception of the managerial ability of executives by outside concerned groups is an example of such external forces. What these groups think of (a) the overall performance of managers, known as organizational effectiveness, and (b) their social performance may affect the compensation-setting board in their executive compensation decision. In essence, this thesis is consistent with the view that in addition to the internal control mechanisms of the corporation, external perceptions, such as organizational effectiveness and social performance, are taken into account in the determination of executive compensation.

This chapter provides an empirical evaluation of the impact of organizational and social performance on executive compensation. The next section develops four hypotheses about executive compensation on the one hand and organizational effectiveness, social performance, size, and profitability on the other hand. These hypotheses state that the level of executive compensation is a positive function of organization effectiveness, social performance, size of the firm, and level of profit in a particular year. All the hypotheses with the exception of the impact of social performance are supported.

## ALTERNATIVE HYPOTHESES

This section introduces four testable hypotheses about compensation and control of top management by a board or directors. The hypotheses concern the relationship between firm size and management compensation; firm financial performance and management compensation; organizational effectiveness and management compensation; and social performance and executive compensation.

### Firm Size and Management Compensation

Most studies examining the determinants of executive compensation indicate that executive compensation is positively correlated with size. Size is generally measured as sales. This evidence shows that the compensation-setting board sets compensation on the basis of size with the rationale that higher compensation is necessary for larger firms whose management involves more complex and demanding tasks. Therefore, the first hypothesis is as follows:

$H_1$: The executive compensation decisions of boards produce a positive correlation between the sales and executive compensation in a given year.

While Murphy[5] presents evidence linking executive compensation and sales growth, this hypothesis extends the thesis by linking the level of executive compensation in a given year to the level of sales in that particular year.

## Firm Profitability and Management Compensation

There is ample evidence indicating a relationship between firm profitability and management compensation. This evidence shows that the executive compensation committee of the board of directors, in their search for incentive arrangements that encourage management to act in the shareholders' interest, sets compensation on the basis of financial performance as measured by profit or rate of return on assets. This is also consistent with the evidence indicating that the compensation plans approved by boards of directors generally link pay to performance measures that are themselves directly related to shareholder wealth. One such performance measure is the profit of the firm. Therefore, the second hypothesis is as follows:

$H_2$: The executive compensation decisions of boards produce a positive correlation between firm profit and executive compensation in a given year.

This hypothesis is in direct conflict (a) with Marris,[6] who asserts that a CEO is more concerned with the size of growth rate of the firm than with its profitability, and (b) with Loomis,[7] who claims that there is no link between compensation and any measure of profitability or stock price performance. This hypothesis, added to the first hypothesis in this chapter, points to both size as measured by sales and performance as measured by profit as key variables considered by the compensation-setting board rather than competing variables in explaining the level of executive compensation as expressed in the neoclassical managerialist debate and earlier empirical studies.

### Organizational Effectiveness and Executive Compensation

Outside groups (shareholders, executives from other firms, watchdog groups, etc.) monitor the performance of managers of a given firm and organize their relationship with that firm (investing in, purchasing from, supply to, etc.) in terms of their perception of the effectiveness of the managerial ability of the firm. This perception, known as organizational effectiveness, has also been termed participant satisfaction, ecological model, or external effectiveness domain.[8-10] There are three major schools of thought on organizational effectiveness: the goal-attainment model, focusing on organizational ends as effectiveness criteria; the systems model, focusing on the means necessary for assuring organizational persistence; and the ecological model, incorporating the interests of internal and external groups. Unlike the other two models, which attempt to produce a single effectiveness statement for a given organization, the ecological model proposes a multiconstituency view of effectiveness. The view treats organizations as systems generating differential assessments of effectiveness by different constituencies.[11] The approach, following suggestions by Scott[12] and Ullman,[13] consists of (a) choosing one constituency, (b) measuring the members' satisfaction using different measures, and (c) combining the results on each measure to develop an overall index so that firms can be ranked in terms of their overall organizational effectiveness. Such a measure of overall effectiveness as viewed by one constituency will create pressure on the compensation-setting board, as it provides the perception by an important outside group of the overall performance of managers. Conscious of the impact of this outside group decision on the survival of the firm, the compensation-setting board will use the measure of overall effectiveness as an input for setting the level of executive compensation. Therefore, the third hypothesis is:

H₃:  The executive compensation decisions of boards produce a positive correlation between organizational effectiveness and executive compensation in a given year.

### Social Performance and Executive Compensation

The relationship between economic performance and social performance has been postulated to include either (a) a positive correlation implying either that economically sound firms can afford the luxury of above-average social performance or that management is responding to the multiple demands emanating from the various constituencies, or (b) a negative correlation given the high expenditures required to attain a high level of social performance.

If the relationship between economic performance and social performance is effectively positive and the board feels it is important to respond to the multiple demands emanating from various constituencies, then compensation-setting boards would link pay to social performance measures. Therefore, the fourth hypothesis is:

$H_4$:   The executive compensation decisions of boards produce a positive correlation between social performance and executive compensation in a given year.

A rejection of this hypothesis would indicate either (a) a negative correlation between economic and social performance, or (b) a failure or a refusal of the board to respond to social demands emanating from various concerned constituencies.

## EMPIRICAL ANALYSIS

### Specification and Measurement of Variables

The hypotheses focus on the relationship between executive compensation on the one hand and organizational effectiveness, social performance, size, and profitability on the other hand. Those variables are defined and measured as follows:

1. Executive compensation is measured as either (a) cash salary plus bonus compensation or (b) cash salary plus bonus plus long-term compensation for the year 1986.
2. Organizational effectiveness of a firm is the 1986 combined score obtained by asking executives, directors, and analysts in the particular industry to rate the company on the following eight key attributes of reputation: (1) quality of management, (2) quality of products/service offered, (3) innovativeness, (4) value as a long-term investment, (5) soundness of financial position, (6) ability to attract/develop/keep talented people, (7) responsibility to the community/environment, and (8) wise use of cor-

porate assets. The survey, conducted by Endos and Morgan, Inc., covered 292 companies in 31 industries and involved 8,000 executives, outside directors, and financial analysts with a 50 percent response rate.[14] Ratings were on a scale of 0 (poor) to 10 (excellent). This 1986 combined score meets the multiple-constituency ecological model view of organizational effectiveness.

3. Social performance of each company is measured by the score obtained in item 7 of the organizational effectiveness instrument, namely, responsibility to the community/environment.

4. The size factor was measured by the 1986 sales amount.

5. The profitability factor was measured by the 1986 net profit amount.

The year 1986 was chosen as the test period because of the availability of data on the organizational effectiveness factor in that particular year.

## The Model

The structure of the model is similar to that advanced by Boyes and Schlagenhauf,[15] who indicated that the log-linear transformation of the compensation income and other data performs as well as the generalized Box-Cox transformation. The basic model is:

$$LnP_i = \beta_0 + \beta_1 LnINC + \beta_2 OE + \beta_3 SP + \beta_4 LnSALES + e_i$$

where:

$P_i$ = Dependent variable, $i$ = 1, 2;

1 = (Cash salary + bonus);

2 = (Cash salary + bonus + long-term compensation);

INC = Net income for the year;

OE = Organizational effectiveness;

SP = Social performance;

SALES = Sales for the year;

0 = Intercept term;

$\beta_0, \beta_1, \beta_2, \beta_3, \beta_4$ = Coefficients for the INC, OE, SP, and SALES;

$e_i$ = Error term;

Ln = Natural log.

## The Sample

The following data requirements were imposed on the selection process for the firms: (a) each company was rated on organizational effectiveness and social performance in 1986, (b) each company was currently (in 1986) listed on Compustat in order to obtain sales and assets data, and (c) executives' pay were available for each company for the year 1986 in their annual report, 10K report, or *Business Week* executive pay survey.[16] The final sample consisted of 155 firms from 28 industries (Exhibit 4.1).

## Regression Results

The results for the model are shown in Exhibit 4.2 using as dependent variables (a) either salary plus bonus or (b) salary plus bonus plus long-term compensation. As shown in both cases, heteroscedasticity in the residuals was observed after using the Glejser test.[17] Nevertheless, all the independent variables were found to be significant with the predicted sign with one exception. The exception is the negative coefficient obtained for the social performance factor.

To correct for heteroscedasticity a weighted least squares was used. Deflating the variables of executive compensation, size, and profits by the logarithm of total assets and then applying OLS is equivalent to using a weighted least square. This transformation yielded the following model:

$$\text{Ln } P_i/\text{LnA} = b_0 \, (1/\text{LnA}) + b_1\text{LnINC/LnA} + b_2\text{OE} + b_3\text{SP} + b_4\text{LnSales/LnA} + u_i$$

where:

LnA = Logarithm of total assets.

The results of the regression using the new form of the model are presented in Exhibit 4.3. As shown, there were drastic improvements in the significance of the regression and in the adjusted $R^2$ values. At the same time the independent variables were found to be significant with

**Exhibit 4.1**
**Sample of Companies Used in the Study**

| Name | Industry |
| --- | --- |
| Boeing | Aerospace |
| Rockwell International | Aerospace |
| General Dynamics | Aerospace |
| Lockheed | Aerospace |
| Martin Marietta | Aerospace |
| McDonnell Douglas | Aerospace |
| Northrop | Aerospace |
| Textron | Aerospace |
| United Technologies | Aerospace |
| AMAX | Mining, Crude-Oil |
| Standard Oil | Mining, Crude-Oil |
| Freeport-McMoran | Mining, Crude-Oil |
| Vulcan Materials | Mining, Crude-Oil |
| Archer Daniels Midland | Food |
| Borden | Food |
| CPC International | Food |
| General Mills | Food |
| Ralston Purina | Food |
| Sara Lee Corporation | Food |
| American Brands | Tobacco |
| Philip Morris | Tobacco |
| Armstrong World Industries | Textiles, Vinyl Flooring |
| Burlington Industries | Textiles, Vinyl Flooring |
| Gulf & Western Industries | Textiles, Vinyl Flooring |
| VF | Textiles, Vinyl Flooring |
| Boise Cascade | Paper, Fiber and Wood Products |
| Georgia-Pacific | Paper, Fiber and Wood Products |
| International Paper | Paper, Fiber and Wood Products |
| Kimberly-Clark | Paper, Fiber and Wood Products |
| Mead | Paper, Fiber and Wood Products |
| Scott Paper | Paper, Fiber and Wood Products |
| Weyerhaeuser | Paper, Fiber and Wood Products |
| R.R. Donnelley & Sons | Publishing, Printing |
| Dow Jones | Publishing, Printing |
| Gannett | Publishing, Printing |
| Knight-Ridder Newspapers | Publishing, Printing |
| McGraw-Hill | Publishing, Printing |
| New York Times | Publishing, Printing |
| Time, Inc. | Publishing, Printing |
| Times Mirror | Publishing, Printing |
| Washington Post | Publishing, Printing |
| Allied | Chemicals |
| American Cyanamid | Chemicals |
| E.I. DuPont De Nemours | Chemicals |

*Source*: Ahmed Riahi-Belkaoui, "Executive Compensation, Organizational Effectiveness, Social Performance and Firm Performance: An Empirical Investigation," *Journal of Business Finance & Accounting* 19, no. 1 (January 1992), pp. 31–34. Reprinted with permission from the *Journal of Business Finance & Accounting*.

**Exhibit 4.1 (continued)**

| Name | Industry |
|------|----------|
| Hercules | Chemicals |
| Monsanto | Chemicals |
| Union Carbide | Chemicals |
| Amoco | Petroleum Refining |
| Atlantic Richfield | Petroleum Refining |
| Chevron | Petroleum Refining |
| Mobil | Petroleum Refining |
| Phillips Petroleum | Petroleum Refining |
| Tenneco | Petroleum Refining |
| U.S. Steel | Petroleum Refining |
| Copper Tire & Rubber | Rubber, Plastic Products |
| Firestone Tire & Rubber | Rubber, Plastic Products |
| Gencorp | Rubber, Plastic Products |
| B.F. Goodrich | Rubber, Plastic Products |
| Corning Glass Works | Glass, Concrete, Abrasives |
| PPG Industries | Gypsum |
| Reynolds Metals | Metal Manufacturing |
| American Can | Metal Products |
| Ball | Metal Products |
| Gilette | Metal Products |
| Parket Hannifin | Metal Products |
| Stanley-Works | Metal Products |
| American Telephone & Telegraph | Electronics, Appliances |
| Emerson Electric | Electronics, Appliances |
| General Electric | Electronics, Appliances |
| ITT | Electronics, Appliances |
| Litton Industries | Electronics, Appliances |
| Motorola | Electronics, Appliances |
| North American Philips | Electronics, Appliances |
| Texas Instruments | Electronics, Appliances |
| Westinghouse Electric | Electronics, Appliances |
| American Standard | Ship Building, Railroad and Transportation Equipment |
| Becton Dickinson | Measuring, Scientific and Photographic Equipment |
| EG & G | Measuring, Scientific and Photographic Equipment |
| Eastman Kodak | Measuring, Scientific and Photographic Equipment |
| General Signal | Measuring, Scientific and Photographic Equipment |
| Perkin-Elmer | Measuring, Scientific and Photographic Equipment |

**Exhibit 4.1** (continued)

| Name | Industry |
| --- | --- |
| Polaroid | Measuring, Scientific and Photographic Equipment |
| Textronix | Measuring, Scientific and Photographic Equipment |
| Borg-Warner | Motor Vehicles and Equipment |
| Dana | Motor Vehicles and Equipment |
| Ford Motor | Motor Vehicles and Equipment |
| General Motors | Motor Vehicles and Equipment |
| TRW | Motor Vehicles and Equipment |
| Abbott Laboratories | Pharmaceuticals |
| American Home Products | Pharmaceuticals |
| Bristol-Myers | Pharmaceuticals |
| Johnson & Johnson | Pharmaceuticals |
| Eli Lilly | Pharmaceuticals |
| Pfizer | Pharmaceuticals |
| Smithkline Beckman | Pharmaceuticals |
| Warner-Lambert | Pharmaceuticals |
| Avon | Soap, Cosmetics |
| Clorox | Soap, Cosmetics |
| Colgate-Palmolive | Soap, Cosmetics |
| International Flavors & Fragrances | Soap, Cosmetics |
| Procter & Gamble | Soap, Cosmetics |
| Control Data | Office Equipment (including Computers) |
| Digital Equipment | Office Equipment |
| Honeywell | Office Equipment |
| IBM | Office Equipment |
| NCR | Office Equipment |
| Pitney Bowes | Office Equipment |
| Wang Laboratories | Office Equipment |
| Caterpillar Tractor | Industrial and Farm Equipment |
| Teledyne | Industrial and Farm Equipment |
| Combustion Engineering | Industrial and Farm Equipment |
| Cummins Engine | Industrial and Farm Equipment |
| Deere | Industrial and Farm Equipment |
| Emhart | Industrial and Farm Equipment |
| Ingersoll-Rand | Industrial and Farm Equipment |
| Anheuser-Busch | Beverages |
| Coca-Cola | Beverages |
| General Cinema | Beverages |
| Pepsico | Beverages |
| CBS | Diversified Service Companies |
| Fluor | Diversified Service Companies |

**Exhibit 4.1 (continued)**

| Name | Industry |
| --- | --- |
| Halliburton | Diversified Service Companies |
| Aetna Life & Casualty | Diversified Service Companies |
| American Express | Diversified Service Companies |
| First Boston | Diversified Service Companies |
| Merrill Lynch | Diversified Service Companies |
| Travelers Corp. | Diversified Service Companies |
| Bankers Trust New York Corp. | Commercial Banking |
| Chase Manhattan Corp. | Commercial Banking |
| Chemical New York Corp. | Commercial Banking |
| Citicorp | Commercial Banking |
| First Chicago Corp. | Commercial Banking |
| Manufacturers Hanover | Commercial Banking |
| J.P. Morgan & Co. | Commercial Banking |
| Security Pacific Corp. | Commercial Banking |
| Household International | Retailing |
| Sears Roebuck | Retailing |
| Southland | Retailing |
| Ameritech | Utilities |
| Bell Atlantic | Utilities |
| Bellsouth | Utilities |
| GTE | Utilities |
| Nynex | Utilities |
| Pacific Gas & Electric | Utilities |
| Pacific Telesis Group | Utilities |
| Southern | Utilities |
| Southwestern Bell | Utilities |
| U.S. West | Utilities |
| Burlington Northern | Transportation |
| CSX | Transportation |
| Delta Airlines | Transportation |
| Santa Fe Southern Pacific | Transportation |
| United Airlines | Transportation |
| Union Pacific | Transportation |

the correct sign with the exception of social performance, which had a negative sign. Based on these results it appears that the executive compensation computed as either salary plus bonus or salary plus bonus plus long-term compensation is positively related to size, profitability, and organizational effectiveness and negatively related to social performance. In terms of the four hypotheses stated earlier, it appears that the executive compensation decisions of boards produce a positive correlation between

**Exhibit 4.2**
**Regression Results**

| Independent Variable | Dependent Variable (in logarithm) | |
| --- | --- | --- |
| | (Salary + Bonus) 1986 | (Salary + Bonus + Long Term Compensation) 1986 |
| Intercept | 4.3410 | 4.193 |
| | (13.659)* | (9.444)* |
| Ln(Profit) | 0.1131 | 0.1082 |
| | (2.887)** | (1.977)** |
| Organizational | 0.0897 | 0.0875 |
| Effectiveness | (3.681)* | (2.569)* |
| Social Performance | −0.1414 | −0.1551 |
| | (−5.457) | (−4.282)* |
| Ln(Sales) | 0.0921 | 0.1353 |
| | (2.091)** | (2.199)* |
| F | 16.372* | 10.540* |
| $R^2$ (Adjusted) | 0.2935 | 0.2050 |
| Heteroscedasticity | Yes ($p < 0.05$) | Yes ($p < 0.05$) |

\* Significant at = 0.01.
\** Significant at = 0.05.

Source: Ahmed Riahi-Belkaoui, "Executive Compensation, Organizational Effectiveness, Social Performance and Firm Performance: An Empirical Investigation," *Journal of Business Finance & Accounting* 19, no. 1 (January 1992), p. 35. Reprinted with permission from the *Journal of Business Finance & Accounting.*

executive compensation on the one hand, and profit, size, and organizational effectiveness on the other hand. Social performance does not appear to be a major external force considered by the executive compensation committee.

## DISCUSSION AND LIMITATION

Results of this chapter provide additional evidence regarding linkages between executive performance and executive compensation. Findings revealed both a significant effect of internal and external control mechanisms available to the compensation committee boards upon executive compensation. Internal control mechanisms based on profit and sales had a significant impact upon compensation. Both sales to assets and profits to assets were significantly related to compensation, providing additional evidence in the ongoing debate about the relative significance of both measures of performance. The significance of both measures confirms

**Exhibit 4.3**
**Regression Results Using Weighted Least Squares**

| Independent Variable | Dependent Variable (in logarithm) | |
|---|---|---|
| | (Salary + Bonus) 1986 | (Salary + Bonus + Long Term Compensation) 1986 |
| Intercept | −0.0388 | −0.0379 |
| | (−0.736) | (−0.605) |
| Ln (Profit/Total | 0.2157 | 0.2101 |
| Assets) | (3.641)* | (2.987)* |
| Organizational | 0.0082 | 0.0080 |
| Effectiveness | (2.318)* | (1.986)** |
| Social Performance | −0.0196 | −0.0208 |
| | (−5.024)* | (−4.503)* |
| Ln (Sales/Total | 0.5299 | 0.5570 |
| Assets | (8.663) | (7.670)* |
| F | 43.275* | 32.791* |
| $R^2$ (Adjusted) | 0.5333 | 0.4621 |

\* Significant at − 0.01.
\*\* Significant at = 0.05.

Source: Ahmed Riahi-Belkaoui, "Executive Compensation, Organizational Effectiveness, Social Performance and Firm Performance: An Empirical Investigation," *Journal of Business Finance & Accounting* 19, no. 1 (January 1992), p. 35. Reprinted with permission from the *Journal of Business Finance & Accounting*.

earlier findings of their joint impact upon executive compensation.[18] Partially linking compensation to sales growth protects the executives from the vagaries of the stock price movements. The results also provide additional evidence pertinent to manager-shareholder incentive compatibility issues. To the extent that executive compensation is positively and significantly associated with corporate sales and earnings, shareholder and managerial interests should be better aligned.

In addition to the internal control mechanisms, executive compensation was found to be positively associated with external perceptions of industry analysts and executives, regarding firm organizational effectiveness. These results provide additional evidence that executives are rewarded for perceived performance beyond defined historical financial measures. External information signals obtained from the managerial labor market with respect to executive performance are significantly related to firm compensation decisions. Interestingly, the significant negative relationship between external perceptions of firm social performance and executive compensation suggests that executives may be penalized for such activities.

Several limitations should be noted in interpreting the results. First, due to data restrictions, as the measures of organizational effectiveness and social performance were only available for 1986, the analysis was limited to a cross-sectional approach. Assuming future availability of data on organizational effectiveness, time series analysis may be used to verify the findings. Second, the measure of organizational effectiveness was computed in the survey as a sum of the eight key attributes of reputation. While there is no a priori justification for a differential weighing of these eight attributes, it is conceivable that an alternative weighing of these eight attributes of organizational effectiveness could yield different results. Future research should extend the findings in light of the above limitations.

## NOTES

1. This chapter has been adapted from Ahmed Riahi-Belkaoui, "Executive Compensation, Organizational Effectiveness, Social Performance and Firm Performance: An Empirical Investigation," *Journal of Business Finance & Accounting* 19, no. 1 (January 1992), pp. 25–38. Reprinted with permission from the *Journal of Business Finance & Accounting*.

2. W. J. Baumol, *Business Behavior, Value, and Growth* (New York: Harcourt, Brace & World, 1967).

3. A. T. Coughlan and R. M. Schmidt, "Executive Compensation, Management Turnover, and Firm Performance: An Empirical Investigation," *Journal of Accounting and Economics* (April 1985), pp. 43–66.

4. Hogan, T. D. and L. R. McPheters (1980). "Executive Compensation: Performance versus Personal Characteristics," *Southern Economics Journal*, Vol. 46 (1980), pp. 1060–1068.

5. K. J. Murphy, "Corporate Performance and Managerial Remuneration: An Empirical Analysis," *Journal of Accounting and Economics* (April 1985), pp. 11–42.

6. R. Marris, "A Model of the Managerial Enterprise," *Quarterly Journal of Economics* 27 (1963), pp. 185–209.

7. C. J. Loomis, "The Madness of Executive Compensation," *Fortune* (July 12, 1982), pp. 42–52.

8. M. A. Keely, "Social Justice Approach to Organizational Evaluation," *Administration Science Quarterly* 23 (1978), pp. 272–292.

9. R. H. Kilman and R. P. Herden, "Towards a Systematic Methodology for Evaluating the Impact of Interventions on Organizational Effectiveness," *Academy of Management Review*, 1, no. 3 (1976), pp. 87–98.

10. R. H. Miles, *Macro-Organizational Behavior* (Glenview, Ill.: Scott, Foresman, 1980).

11. T. Connolly, E. J. Conlon, and S. J. Deutsh, "Organizational Effectiveness: A Multiple-Constituency Approach," *Academy of Management Review* 5, no. 2 (1980), p. 214.

12. W. R. Scott, *Organizations: Rational, Natural and Operational Systems* (Englewood Cliffs, N.J.: Prentice-Hall, 1981), p. 323.

13. A. A. Ullman, "Data in Search for a Theory: A Critical Examination of the Relationship among Social Performance, Social Disclosure and Economic Performance of U.S. Firms," *The Academy of Management Review* (July 1985), p. 543.

14. C. Hutton, "America's Most Admired Corporation," *Fortune* (January 6, 1986), pp. 16–27.

15. W. J. Boyes and D. E. Schlagenhauf, "Managerial Incentives and the Specification of Function Forms," *Southern Economic Journal* (April 1979), pp. 1225–1232.

16. J. A. Byrne, "Executive Pay: Who Got What in '86," *Business Week* (May 4, 1987), pp. 50–94.

17. J. Johnston, *Economic Methods* (New York: McGraw-Hill, 1972), p. 220.

18. S. Baker, "Executive Incomes, Profit and Revenues: A Comment on Functional Specification," *Southern Economic Journal* (April 1969), pp. 379–383.

## SELECTED READINGS

Abdel-Khalik, A. R. "The Effect of LIFO-Switching and Firm Ownership on Executives' Pay." *Journal of Accounting Research* 23 (1985), pp. 427–447.

Alexander, G. J., and R. A. Buchholz. "Corporate Social Responsibility and Stock Market Performance." *Academy of Management Journal* 21 (1978), pp. 479–486.

Antle, R., and A. Smith. "An Empirical Investigation into Relative Performance Evaluation of Corporate Executives." *Journal of Accounting Research* (Spring 1986), pp. 1–39.

Baker, S. "Executive Incomes, Profit and Revenues: A Comment on Functional Specification." *Southern Economic Journal* (April 1969), pp. 379–383.

Baumol, W. J. *Business Behavior, Value, and Growth.* New York: Harcourt, Brace & World, 1967.

Benston, G. J. "The Self-Serving Management Hypothesis: Some Evidence." *Journal of Accounting and Economics* (April 1985), pp. 67–84.

Bowman, E. H., and M. Haire. "A Strategic Posture toward Corporate Social Responsibility." *California Management Review* 18, no. 2 (1985), pp. 49–58.

Boyes, W. J., and D. E. Schlagenhauf. "Managerial Incentives and the Specification of Functional Forms." *Southern Economic Journal* (April 1979), pp. 1225–1232.

Bragdon, J. H., and J. A. T. Marlin. "Is Pollution Profitable?" *Risk Management* 19, no. 4 (1979), pp. 9–18.

Byrne, J. A. "Executive Pay: Who Got What in '86." *Business Week* (May 4, 1987), pp. 50–94.

Chen, K. H., and R. W. Metcalf. "The Relationship between Pollution Control and Financial Indicators Revisited." *The Accounting Review* (January 1980), pp. 168–177.

Ciscel, D. H., and T. M. Carroll. "The Determinants of Executive Salaries: An Econometric Survey." *Review of Economics and Statistics* (February 1980), pp. 7–13.

Cochran, P. L., and R. A. Wood. "Corporate Social Responsibility and Financial Performance." *Academy of Management Journal* 27 (1984), pp. 42–56.

Commons, M. S. *Basic Econometrics*. London: Longman, 1976.

Connolly, T., E. J. Conlon, and S. J. Deutsh. "Organizational Effectiveness: A Multiple-Constituency Approach." *Academy of Management Review* 5, no. 2 (1980), pp. 211–217.

Cosh, A. "The Remuneration of Chief Executives in the United Kingdom." *Economic Journal* 85 (1975), pp. 75–94.

Coughlan, A. T., and R. M. Schmidt. "Executive Compensation, Management Turnover, and Firm Performance: An Empirical Investigation." *Journal of Accounting and Economics* (April 1985), pp. 43–66.

Folger, H. R., and F. Nutt. "A Note on Social Responsibility and Stock Valuation." *Academy of Management Journal* 18 (1975), pp. 155–160.

Fox, H. "Top Executive Compensation: 1978." New York: The Conference Board, 1980.

Healy, P. M., S. H. Kang, and K. G. Palepu. "The Effect of Accounting Procedure Changes on CEO's Cash Salary and Bonus Compensation." *Journal of Accounting and Economics* (April 1987), pp. 7–34.

Hewley, P. M. "The Effect of Bonus Schemes on Accounting Decisions." *Journal of Accounting and Economics* (April 1985), pp. 85–108.

Hirschey, M., and J. L. Pappas. "Regulatory and Life Cycle Influences of Managerial Incentives." *Southern Economic Journal* 48 (1981), pp. 327–334.

Hogan, T. D., and L. R. McPheters. "Executive Compensation: Performance versus Personal Characteristics." *Southern Economics Journal* 46 (1980), pp. 1060–1068.

Hutton, C. "America's Most Admired Corporation." *Fortune* (January 6, 1986), pp. 16–27.

Johnston, J. *Economic Methods*. New York: McGraw-Hill, 1972.

Kedia, B. L., and E. C. Kuntz. "The Context of Social Performance: An Empirical Study of Texas Banks." In L. E. Preston, ed., *Research in Cor-*

porate Social Performance and Policy, Vol. 3. Greenwich, Conn.: JAI Press, 1981: pp. 133–154.

Keeley, M. A. "Social Justice Approach to Organizational Evaluation." *Administration Science Quarterly* 23 (1978), pp. 272–292.

Kilman, R. H., and R. P. Herden. "Towards a Systematic Methodology for Evaluating the Impact of Interventions on Organizational Effectiveness." *Academy of Management Review* 1, no. 3 (1976), pp. 87–98.

Lewellen, W. G., and B. Huntsman. "Managerial Pay and Corporate Performance." *American Economic Review* 60 (1970), pp. 710–720.

Loomis, C. J. "The Madness of Executive Compensation." *Fortune* (July 12, 1982), pp. 42–52.

Marris, R. "A Model of the Managerial Enterprise." *Quarterly Journal of Economics* 27 (1963), pp. 185–209.

McGuire, J. W., J. S. W. Chiu, and A. O. Elbing. "Executive Income Sales and Profits." *American Economic Review* 57 (1962), pp. 753–761.

Masson, R. T. "Executive Motivations, Earnings, and Consequent Equity Performance." *Journal of Political Economy* 79 (1971), pp. 1278–1292.

Mecks, G., and G. Whittington. "Directors' Pay, Growth and Profitability." *Journal of Industrial Economy* 4 (1981), 234–252.

Miles, R. H. *Macro-Organizational Behavior*. Glenview, Ill.: Scott, Foresman, 1980.

Moskowitz, P. "Choosing Socially Responsible Stocks." *Business and Society Review* 1 (1975), pp. 71–75.

Murphy, K. J. "Corporate Performance and Managerial Remuneration: An Empirical Analysis." *Journal of Accounting and Economics* (April 1985), pp. 11–42.

Neter, H., and W. Wasserman. *Applied Linear Statistical Methods*. Homewood, Ill.: Irwin, 1974.

Parket, I. R., and H. Eilbirt. "Social Responsibility: Underlying Factors." *Business Horizons* 18, no. 4 (1975), pp. 5–10.

Price, J. L. "The Study of Organizational Effectiveness." *Sociological Quarterly* 13 (1972), pp. 3–15.

Ramanathan, K. V. "Toward a Theory of Corporate Social Accounting." *The Accounting Review* (July 1976), pp. 516–528.

Rich, J. T., and J. A. Larson. "Why Some Long-Term Incentives Fail." *Compensation Review* 16, no. 1 (1984), pp. 26–37.

Scott, W. R. *Organizations: Rational, Natural and Operational Systems*. Englewood Cliffs, N.J.: Prentice-Hall, 1981.

Spicer, B. H. "Investors, Corporate Social Performance and Information Disclosure: An Empirical Study." *The Accounting Review* (January 1978), pp. 94–111.

———. "Market Risk, Accounting Data and Companies' Pollution Control Records." *Journal of Business Finance and Accounting* 5, no. 1 (Spring 1978), pp. 67–83.

Sturdivant, F. D., and J. L. Ginter. "Corporate Social Responsiveness, Management Attitudes and Economic Performance, Social Disclosure and Economic Performance of U.S. Firms." *California Management Review* (1977), pp. 30–39.

Ullman, A. A. "Data in Search for a Theory: A Critical Examination of the Relationship among Social Performance, Social Disclosure and Economic Performance of U.S. Firms." *The Academy of Management Review* (July 1985), pp. 540–557.

Vance, S. C. "Are Socially Responsible Corporations Good Investment Risks?" *Management Review* 64, no. 8 (1975), pp. 15–24.

# 5

## Financial Outcomes of Corporate Effectiveness: The Impact on Asset Management Performance

### INTRODUCTION[1]

The reputation of a firm is important for various decisions ranging from resource allocation and career decisions to product choices, to name only a few.[2] It is an important signal of the firm's organizational effectiveness. Favorable reputations can create favorable situations for firms that include (a) the generation of excess returns by inhibiting the mobility of rivals in an industry;[3] (b) the capability of charging premium prices to consumers;[4] and (c) the creation of a better image in the capital markets and to investors.[5]

With two exceptions, most previous empirical investigations have examined the relationship between earnings performance and social performance.[6] Two studies, however, investigated the relationship between reputation and various economic and noneconomic criteria that may be used by corporate audiences to construct reputations.[7,8] Although the signals used in these two studies show attendance by corporate audiences to different information cues, we propose that of most importance to these parties are signals about asset management performance. We therefore propose specific hypotheses relating assessments of reputation to various information signals about a firm's asset management performance, specifically using accounting and market signals that indicate size of assets, market assessment of the value of the assets in place, asset turnover, and profit margin.

## RELATED RESEARCH

Two studies have investigated the determinants of reputation building. Based on the thesis that an organization's social performance is an indistinguishable component of its effectiveness,[9] Belkaoui and Pavlik expanded the definition of social performance to include organizational effectiveness, and investigated the relationship between organizational effectiveness and economic performance. Following the ecological model, organizational effectiveness by constructs' reputational ranking of firms was used. The reputational rankings were found to be positively related to profitability, size, and price/earnings ratios and negatively related to systematic risk.

Using a similar approach, Fombrun and Shanley[10] found the same reputational rankings, for a different period and a different sample, to be related to the firms' risk-return profiles, resource allocations, social responsiveness, institutional ownership, media exposure, and corporate diversification. These all signal constituents about firms' projects and generate reputations.

This chapter differs by its focus on linking reputational rankings specifically to asset management performance, as this is the most salient issue in evaluating corporate performance.

## REPUTATION BUILDING

### Objective Function and Stewardship

This chapter hypothesizes that corporate audiences attend to different features of firms' asset management performance in constructing reputational rankings. The focus on asset management performance rather than on other attributes of firm performance results from specific expectations of corporate audiences about the objective function of management and the nature of asset stewardship.

Organizations are social units deliberately constructed and reconstructed to seek specific goals. J. D. Thompson[11] differentiated between goals *held for* an organization and goals *of* an organization. The former goals are held by outside members of the organization who have a given interest in the activities of the firm, while the latter are the goals held by persons and/or managers who are part of the "dominant coalition" in terms of holding enough control to commit the organization to a given direction. The same distinction is made by Perrow[12] as official goals versus operative goals. The main difference between goals arises when the official goals held by corporate audiences conform to a shareholder-wealth-maximization model and the operative goals conform to a managerial-welfare-maximization model.[13] The shareholder-wealth-maximization model holds that the operative goals are to maximize the wealth of stockholders. The firm accepts all projects yielding more than the cost of capital and therefore is only interested in an efficient use of the assets of the firm. The management-welfare-maximization model holds that managers run firms for their own benefit. It follows that corporate audiences committed to a shareholder-wealth-maximization view of operative goals will construct reputations on the basis of information about firms' asset management performance.

The stewardship concept is basically a feature of the principal-agent relationship, whereby the agent is assumed to safeguard the resources of the principal. The stewardship concept has evolved over time. Birnberg[14] distinguished four periods: (1) the pure-custodial period; (2) the traditional-custodial period; (3) the asset-utilization period; and (4) the open-ended period. The first two periods refer to the need for the agent to return the resources intact to the principal by performing minimal tasks to fulfill the custodial function. The third period refers to the need for the agent to provide initiative and insight in using the assets to conform to agreed-upon plans. Finally, the open-ended period differs from the asset-utilization period by providing more flexibility in the use of assets and enabling the agent to chart the course of asset utilization. The third and fourth periods are more reflective of the contemporary conception of stewardship. It follows that corporate audiences holding these views of stewardship will construct reputations on the basis of information about firms' asset management performance.

## Interpreting Ambiguous Signals about Asset Management

Based on the shareholder-wealth-maximization model for operative goals of firms, and the asset-utilization and open-ended use of assets for views of stewardship, corporate audiences are assumed to construct reputations on the basis of informational signals about firms' asset management performance. Asset management performance is considered to be

**Exhibit 5.1**
**Model of Reputation Building under Conditions of Incomplete**
**Information about Asset Management Performance**

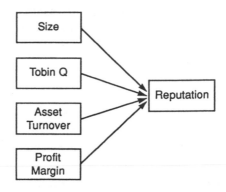

*Source*: Ahmed Riahi-Belkaoui and Ellen Pavlik, ''Asset Management Performance and Reputation
Building for Large US Firms,'' *British Journal of Management* 2 (1991), p. 233. © 1991 by
John Wiley & Sons, Ltd. Reprinted with permission from the *British Journal of Management.*

a combination of asset size, market assessment of the value of assets in
place, asset turnover, and profit margin. Exhibit 5.1 presents the model
linking reputation to these components of asset management performance.

### Size

Large firms are more politically sensitive than small firms. If their
profits are also large, they fear government actions. The amount and
quality of information of large firms will be larger in response to the
increased scrutiny. As a result it may be safe to assume that corporate
audiences will appreciate better the information quality of larger firms
and assign them a better reputation.

$H_1$:   The larger the firm, the better its reputation.

### Tobin Q

Tobin Q, the market value of the firm, divided by the replacement
value of the assets, measures the market's assessment of the value of the
assets in place and the company's future investment opportunities. It is
a measure of managerial performance. It can also be interpreted as a
measure of agency costs. Lang and Litzenberg[15] showed that a Q ratio
below 1:0 is evidence of overinvestment. Jensen[16] argued that over-

investment can be due to conflicts of interest between managers and shareholders over the use of free cash flow generated by the firm. As both a measure of managerial performance and a measure of agency costs, Tobin Q can also be interpreted as a signal of asset management performance.

$H_2$: The greater a firm's Tobin Q, the better its reputation.

### Asset Turnover and Profit Margin

A firm's efficient use of its assets is best reflected by its rate of return on assets. The rate of return on assets is, in fact, a composite measure depending on: (a) the asset turnover as computed by sales over assets, and (b) the profit margin as computed by profit over sales. The profit margin ratio indicates how much of net income is earned from each dollar of sales. The asset turnover ratio indicates how many times annual sales cover total assets. A firm's efficient use of its assets is best accomplished by securing higher values for both ratios or higher values for one of the ratios.

$H_3$: The greater a firm's asset turnover, the better its reputation.

$H_4$: The greater a firm's profit margin, the better its reputation.

## THE MODEL

The four hypotheses may be expressed by the following model:

$$REP_{it} = \alpha_{0t} + \alpha_{1(t-1)} (TA_{(t-1)} - ITA_{(t-1)}) + \alpha_{2(t-1)} + (TQ_{(t-1)} - ITQ_{(t-1)}) + \alpha_{3(t-1)} (AT_{(t-1)} - IAT_{(t-1)}) + \alpha_{4(t-1)} (PM_{(t-1)} - IPM_{(t-1)}) + \varepsilon_{(t-1)}$$

where:

$REP_{1t}$ = Overall score of reputation

$REP_{2t}$ = Score on quality of management

$REP_{3t}$ = Score on quality of products/service offered

$REP_{4t}$ = Score on innovativeness

$REP_{5t}$ = Score on value as a long-term investment

$\text{REP}_{6t}$   = Score on soundness of financial position

$\text{REP}_{7t}$   = Score on ability to attract/develop/keep talented people

$\text{REP}_{8t}$   = Score on responsibility to the community/environment

$\text{REP}_{9t}$   = Score on wise use of corporate assets

$\text{TA}_{(t-1)}$   = Total assets for $(t-1)$

$\text{ITA}_{(t-1)}$   = Average total assets for the industry for $(t-1)$

$\text{TQ}_{(t-1)}$   = Tobin Q for $(t-1)$

$\text{ITQ}_{(t-1)}$   = Average Tobin Q for the industry for $(t-1)$

$\text{AT}_{(t-1)}$   = Asset turnover for $(t-1)$

$\text{IAT}_{(t-1)}$   = Average asset turnover for the industry for $(t-1)$

$\text{PM}_{(t-1)}$   = Profit margin for $(t-1)$

$\text{IPM}_{(t-1)}$   = Average profit margin for the industry for $(t-1)$

The model was run for both $t = 1987$ and $t = 1988$. The independent variables were adjusted for industry averages to control for industry membership.

## THE DATA

### Dependent Variables

The main dependent variable of reputation is the combined score obtained in an annual *Fortune* magazine survey. The *Fortune* survey covers every industry group comprising four or more companies. The industry groups are based on categories established by the U.S. Office of Management and Budget (OMB). Thirty-three industry groupings were included in the 1987 and 1988 surveys, covering, respectively, 300 and 306 firms of different sizes. The survey asked executives, directors, and analysts in particular industries to rate a company on the following eight key attributes of reputation:

1. Quality of management

2. Quality of products/service offered

3. Innovativeness

4. Value as a long-term investment

5. Soundness of financial position

6. Ability to attract/develop/keep talented people

7. Responsibility to the community/environment

8. Wise use of corporate assets

Ratings were on a scale of 0 (poor) to 10 (excellent). The score met the multiple-consistency ecological model view of organization effectiveness. For the purpose of our study, the 1988 and 1987 *Fortune* magazine surveys were used. They contain the overall scores for the firms' rating in 1987 and 1986. The use of the overall score rather than a factor analysis of the eight scores is based on the facts that: (a) it is the overall score that is published in *Fortune* magazine rather than the eight scores on the attribute, and (b) it is then the overall score that is perceived by the readers as well as the respondents of the survey as the reputation index. From previous experience, the respondents know that the means of their scores on the eight attributes will be published as the overall score of reputation.

Besides the overall score, the eight individual scores on the eight key attributes of reputation were also used as dependent variables to evaluate their differential relations with asset management performance.

### Independent Variables

The independent variables include firm size, Tobin Q, asset turnover, and profit margin minus their respective industry average for the year. Size for 1986 and 1987 was computed as the total assets for each of these two years. Tobin Q for 1986 and 1987 was computed as the market value of the firm, divided by the replacement value of the assets measures for each of the two years. Asset turnover for 1986 and 1987 was computed as the total sales divided by the total assets for each of the two years. Profit margin for 1986 and 1987 was computed as the net profit divided by total sales for each of the two years.

### Sample

To ensure the greatest sample of firms for which data would be available for all variables, the initial sample chosen was all the firms included in *Fortune*'s 1987 and 1988 studies of corporate reputation. Accounting data for these firms were obtained from Standard and Poor's COMPUSTAT industrial and business segment tapes. Replacement cost data were determined from the inflation data disclosures in the annual reports resulting from the application of Statement 33. The final sample amounted to 114 firms.

Exhibit 5.2 presents the basic descriptive statistics for all the variables in the model and the intercorrelations among these variables. The low intercorrelations among adjusted predictor variables used in the model gave no reason to suspect multicollinearity, and various diagnostic tests run on derived regression models, where size was expressed as the logarithm of assets, confirmed that it was not a problem.

## RESULTS

Exhibits 5.3 and 5.4 present the results of the regression coefficients for all the independent variables, using all the measures of reputation as dependent variables for both 1987 and 1988.

Hypothesis 1 predicts that asset size will positively affect reputation. With two exceptions, the results for both years corroborate the hypothesis that corporate audiences tend to assign higher (better) reputations to firms with bigger size as measured by total assets. The two exceptions are for reputation measured as quality of products/service offered and innovativeness for both years.

Hypothesis 2 predicts that the market's assessment of the value of the assets in place, and the company's future investment opportunities as measured by Tobin Q, will positively affect reputation. With some exceptions, the results for both years corroborate the hypothesis that corporate audiences tend to assign higher reputations to firms with a higher Tobin Q. The exceptions are for reputation as measured by quality of management in both years and as measured by responsibility to the community/environment in 1987.

Hypothesis 3 predicts that the asset turnover will significantly influence reputational judgments. With two exceptions, the results for both years indicate that corporate audiences tend to assign higher reputations to firms with a high asset turnover ratio. The two exceptions are for reputation as measured by quality of products/service offered and responsibility to the community/environment for both years.

Finally, Hypothesis 4 predicts that the profit margin will positively affect reputation. With no exceptions, the results for both years corroborate the hypothesis that corporate audiences tend to assign higher reputations to firms with a high profit margin ratio.

In short, the overall reputation of firms is positively related to the total assets, Tobin Q, asset turnover, and profit margin of the firm after con-

**Exhibit 5.2**
**Descriptive Statistics**

| Variables | Mean | Standard deviation | Correlations | | | |
| --- | --- | --- | --- | --- | --- | --- |
| | | | 1 | 2 | 3 | 4 |
| Reputation | 6.569 | 0.747 | | | | |
| Assets ($1000s) | 276.609 | 620.790 | 0.150*** | | | |
| Tobin Q | 1.292 | 1.640 | 0.283* | −0.102 | | |
| Asset Turnover | 0.064 | 0.067 | 0.345*1 | −0.060 | 0.203* | |
| Profit margin | 1.247 | 0.544 | 0.079 | −0.136** | 0.120*** | −0.239* |

*Significant at α = 0.01. **Significant at α = 0.05. ***Significant at α = 0.10.

*Source:* Ahmed Riahi-Belkaoui and Ellen Pavlik, "Asset Management Performance and Reputation Building for Large US Firms," *British Journal of Management* 2 (1991), p. 235. © 1991 by John Wiley & Sons, Ltd. Reprinted with permission from the *British Journal of Management.*

**Exhibit 5.3**
**Explaining Corporate Reputation in 1987**

| Independent variables/ Dependent variables | Intercept | TA-ITA | TQ-ITQ | AT-IAT | PM-IPM | F | R² Adj.(%) |
|---|---|---|---|---|---|---|---|
| Overall corporate reputation '87 | 6.474 (94.6) | 0.00001 (94.6)* | 0.1322 (1.883)** | 0.2889 (2.551)* | 5.700 (3.797)* | 8.345* | 23.44 |
| Quality of management | 6.720 (78.3) | 0.00001 (2.085)** | 0.0974 (1.102) | 0.3906 (2.734)* | 5.864 (3.101*) | 5.137* | 15.74 |
| Quality of products/ services offered | 7.131 (105.87)* | 0.000006 (1.296) | 0.1140 (1.642)*** | 0.1697 (1.516) | 3.095 (2.085)** | 3.173* | 10.34 |
| Innovativeness | 6.2367 (76.14)* | 0.000001 (0.321) | 0.1491 (1.766)*** | 0.2715 (1.993)** | 2.8489 (1.677)*** | 2.954** | 9.7* |
| Value as a long-term investment | 6.19 (81.5) | 0.00002 (3.863)* | 0.1302 (1.662)*** | 0.2591 (2.051)** | 7.731 (4.615)* | 11.025* | 28.62 |
| Soundness of financial position | 6.613 (75.8)* | 0.00002 (4.411)* | 0.2060 (2.292)** | 0.4126 (2.845)* | 6.82 (5.628)* | 16.590* | 37.63 |
| Ability to attract/develop/ keep talented people | 6.2917 (83.68) | 0.00001 (3.619)* | 0.1285 (1.658)*** | 0.3438 (2.750)* | 5.8618 (3.536)* | 8.212* | 22.99 |
| Responsibility to community/ environment | 6.3058 (97.054)* | 0.00001 (3.698)* | 0.08866 (1.323) | 0.1621 (1.501) | 3.3274 (2.323)** | 5.310* | 16.18 |
| Wise use of resources | 6.208 (84.22)* | 0.00009 (1.836)** | 0.1411 (1.841)* | 0.2060 (2.387)* | 6.0246 (3.664) | 7.310* | 20.59 |

*Absolute value of *t*-statistic in parenthesis. *Significant at $\alpha = 0.01$. **Significant at $\alpha = 0.05$. ***Significant at $\alpha = 0.10$.

*Source:* Ahmed Riahi-Belkaoui and Ellen Pavlik, "Asset Management Performance and Reputation Building for Large US Firms," *British Journal of Management* 2 (1991), p. 235. © 1991 by John Wiley & Sons, Ltd. Reprinted with permission from the *British Journal of Management*.

**Exhibit 5.4**
**Explaining Corporate Reputation in 1988**

| Independent variables / Dependent variables | Intercept | TA-ITA | TQ-ITQ | AT-IAT | PM-IPM | F | R² Adj.(%) |
|---|---|---|---|---|---|---|---|
| Overall corporate reputation '87 | 6.553 (93.5) | 0.000008 (1.7)*** | 0.2327 (2.640)* | 0.2393 (2.120)** | 6.2643 (3.968)* | 11.535* | 29.36 |
| Quality of management | 6.770 (22.2)* | 0.000003 (2.513)** | 0.1696 (1.543) | 0.34053 (2.419)* | 7.253 (3.686)* | 7.871* | 22.25 |
| Quality of products/ services offered | 7.147 (95.56)* | 0.000001 (0.324) | 0.2540 (2.707)* | 0.1759 (1.465) | 3.3936 (2.020)* | 6.067* | 18.57 |
| Innovativeness | 6.29 (71.30)* | 0.000005 (0.840) | 0.2453 (2.218)* | 0.2400 (1.690)*** | 2.875 (1.452) | 4.688* | 14.56 |
| Value as a long-term investment | 6.360 (78.08)* | 0.000001 (2.375)* | 0.2123 (2.078)** | 0.2126 (1.625)*** | 7.601 (4.155)* | 10.70* | 28.01 |
| Soundness of financial position | 6.73 (76.7)* | 0.00002 (4.043)* | 0.3456 (3.141)* | 0.3335 (2.367)* | 11.421 (5.797)* | 22.49* | 45.00 |
| Ability to attract/develop/ keep talented people | 6.35 (79.19) | 0.00001 (2.451)* | 0.2537 (2.519)* | 0.2871 (2.226)** | 6.667 (3.696)* | 10.575* | 27.77 |
| Responsibility to community/ environment | 6.36 (88.13)* | 0.00001 (3.038)* | 0.1857 (2.049)** | 0.1039 (0.895) | 3.667 (2.259)** | 6.044* | 18.02 |
| Wise use of resources | 6.35 (83.23)* | 0.000006 (0.114) | 0.1952 (2.039)* | 0.1949 (1.690)* | 6.877 (4.013)* | 10.053* | 26.85 |

* Absolute value of $t$-statistic in parenthesis. *Significant at $\alpha = 0.01$. **Significant at $\alpha = 0.05$. ***Significant at $\alpha = 0.10$.

*Source*: Ahmed Riahi-Belkaoui and Ellen Pavlik, "Asset Management Performance and Reputation Building for Large US Firms," *British Journal of Management* 2 (1991), p. 236. © 1991 by John Wiley & Sons, Ltd. Reprinted with permission from the *British Journal of Management*.

trolling for industry averages, as hypothesized. The role of asset management in creating reputation is, however, present and significant to different degrees for each of the eight component scores and for each of the two years examined, showing a persistency for each score and for each year. The best performance by an independent variable is played by the significant role of the profit margin ratio for the total reputation score as well as the eight component scores for both years.

The subdimension regression also offers some interesting results. For example, the quality of management is highly related to asset size, showing an acceptance by external audiences of a managerial wealth maximization technique used by managers, involving the maximization of size. This finding is also verified by the highly significant relationship between wise use of resources and asset size. This points to an interesting congruence between management's objectives and external audiences' assessments.

## DISCUSSION AND CONCLUSIONS

Both the shareholder-wealth maximization model and the open-ended stewardship concept maintain that corporate audiences are very much concerned by managers' use of the assets of the firm. This study had hypothesized that, consequently, corporate audiences will construct reputational rankings on the basis of the asset management performance. More specifically, the results of an empirical study of 114 large U.S. firms supported the general hypothesis that corporate audiences construct reputations on the basis of information about a firm's asset management performance, specifically using market and accounting signals indicating size of assets, market assessment of the value of the assets in place, asset turnover, and profit margin. Given the potential that reputation rankings may crystallize the statuses of firms within an industrial social system, firms, through a thorough understanding of the informational medium from which corporate audiences construct reputations, signal these audiences about their asset management performance through both accounting and market signals.

## NOTES

1. This chapter has been largely adapted from Ahmed Riahi-Belkaoui and Ellen Pavlik, ''Asset Management Performance and Reputation Building for

Large US Firms," *British Journal of Management* 2 (1991), pp. 231–238. ©
1991 by John Wiley & Sons, Ltd. Reprinted with permission from the *British
Journal of Management.*

2. G. R. Dowling, "Managing Your Corporate Images," *Industrial Marketing Management* 15 (1986), pp. 109–115.

3. R. E. Caves and M. E. Porter, "From Entry Barriers to Mobility Barriers," *Quarterly Journal of Economics* 91 (1977), pp. 421–434.

4. B. Klein and K. Leffler, "The Role of Market Forces in Assuring Contractual Performance," *Journal of Political Economy* 85 (1981), pp. 615–641.

5. R. P. Bealty and J. R. Ritter, "Investment Banking, Reputation, and Underpricing of Initial Public Offerings," *Journal of Financial Economics* 15 (1986), pp. 213–232.

6. A. A. Ullman, "Data in Search of a Theory: A Critical Examination of the Relationship among Social Performance, Social Disclosure and Economic Performance of U.S. Firms," *Academy of Management Review* 10 (1985), pp. 540–557.

7. C. J. Fombrun and M. Shanley, "What's in a Name? Reputation Building and Corporate Strategy," *Academy of Management Journal* 33 (1990), pp. 233–258.

8. A. Belkaoui, "Organizational Effectiveness, Social Performance and Economic Performance," *Research in Corporate Social Performance and Policy* 12 (1992).

9. Ahmed Belkaoui and Ellen Pavlik, *Accounting for Corporate Reputation* (Westport, Conn.: Quorum, 1992), 143–153.

10. Fombrun and Shanley, op. cit.

11. J. D. Thompson, *Organizations in Action* (New York: McGraw-Hill, 1967).

12. C. Perrow, "The Analysis of Goals in Complex Organizations," *American Sociological Review* 6 (1961), pp. 854–866.

13. A. Belkaoui, *Conceptual Foundations of Management Accounting* (Reading, Mass.: Addison-Wesley, 1980).

14. J. C. Birnberg, "The Role of Accounting in Financial Disclosure," *Accounting Organizations and Society* (June 1980), pp. 71–80.

15. L. Lang and R. Litzenberg, "What Information Is Contained in the Dividend Announcement?" *Journal of Financial Economics* 6 (1989), pp. 32–67.

16. M. C. Jensen, "Agency Costs of Free Cash Flow, Corporate Finance and Takeovers," *American Economic Review* 76 (1986), pp. 323–329.

## SELECTED READINGS

Bealty, R. P., and J. R. Ritter. "Investment Banking, Reputation, and Underpricing of Initial Public Offerings." *Journal of Financial Economics* 15 (1986), pp. 213–232.

Belkaoui, A. *Conceptual Foundations of Management Accounting*. Reading, Mass.: Addison-Wesley, 1980.

————. "Organizational Effectiveness, Social Performance and Economic Performance." *Research in Corporate Social Performance and Policy* 12 (1992).

Belkaoui, Ahmed, and Ellen Pavlik. *Accounting for Corporate Reputation*. Westport, Conn.: Quorum, 1992, 143–153.

Birnberg, J. C. "The Role of Accounting in Financial Disclosure." *Accounting, Organizations and Society* (June 1980), pp. 71–80.

Caves, R. E., and M. E. Porter. "From Entry Barriers to Mobility Barriers." *Quarterly Journal of Economics* 91 (1977), pp. 421–434.

Dowling, G. R. "Managing Your Corporate Images." *Industrial Marketing Management* 15 (1986), pp. 109–115.

Fombrun, C. J., and M. Shanley. "What's in a Name? Reputation Building and Corporate Strategy." *Academy of Management Journal* 33 (1990), pp. 233–258.

Jensen, M. C. "Agency Costs of Free Cash Flow, Corporate Finance and Takeovers." *American Economic Review* 76 (1986), pp. 323–329.

Klein, B., and K. Leffler. "The Role of Market Forces in Assuring Contractual Performance." *Journal of Political Economy* 85 (1981), pp. 615–641.

Lang, L., and R. Litzenberg. "What Information Is Contained in the Dividend Announcement?" *Journal of Financial Economics* 6 (1989), pp. 32–67.

Perrow, C. "The Analysis of Goals in Complex Organizations." *American Sociological Review* 6 (1961), pp. 854–866.

Thompson, J. D. *Organizations in Action*. New York: McGraw-Hill, 1967.

Ullman, A. A. "Data in Search of a Theory: A Critical Examination of the Relationship among Social Performance, Social Disclosure and Economic Performance of U.S. Firms." *Academy of Management Review* 10 (1985), pp. 540–557.

# 6

## Financial Outcomes of Socio-Economic Accounting: The Financial Determinants of the Social Information Disclosure Decision

### INTRODUCTION[1]

In examining the relationship between disclosure, social performance, and economic performance, the empirical literature to date focuses on the potential relationship between (a) social disclosure and social performance, (b) social disclosure and economic performance based on either accounting or marketing variables, and (c) social performance and economic performance. Depending on the type of conceptualization and operationalization of key variables, the results range from strong correlation to no correlation. The diversity of results may be due to the failure to analyze the relationship among social disclosure, social performance, and economic performance within a single conceptual framework.[2–5]

Accordingly, this chapter develops and empirically tests a positive model of the corporate decision to disclose social information in terms of both social performance and economic performance. In short, the model tests the empirical relationship of social disclosure with both social and economic performance. The related literature is then reviewed. The next section identifies the factors influencing the decision to disclose social information. The variables are then defined before a presentation of the empirical tests. Finally, the summary and conclusion are presented.

## RELATED RESEARCH

Three types of empirical studies characterize the research on the social responsibility accounting of firms.[6]

The first type examines the potential relationships between the extensiveness of a firm's social disclosure and its social performance with the hypothesis that the quantity and the quality of social disclosure are positively correlated with its social performance.[7-13] Social disclosure was measured differently, including (a) social disclosure scale derived from Ernst and Ernst,[14] (b) percentage of prose in annual reports, (c) quality of disclosure in annual reports, and (d) quantity of disclosure in annual reports. Similarly, social performance was measured differently, including (a) reputational scales from *Business and Society Review*,[15,16] (b) Moskowitz[17] reputational scales, citizenship awards, (c) CEP pollution performance index, and (d) student evaluation of industry reputation. Only two studies controlled for size. The results included no correlation in four studies, negative correlation in one study, and positive correlation in two studies.

The second type of study examines the potential relationships between social performance and economic performance, with the hypothesis that social performance and economic performance can be correlated in three ways: positively, negatively, and association between extreme levels.[18-23] The measures of social performance include, in addition to those identified for the first type of studies, a measure based on the existence of social responsibility programs in five different areas.

The economic performance surrogates vary, including (a) measures of stockholder return, (b) measures of rates of return in either equity, assets, sales, or capital, (c) measures of earnings per share, (d) measures of income, and/or (e) measures of price-earning ratios. Three studies controlled for either beta, size, asset age, or asset turnover. The results show partial support for each hypothesis, i.e., no correlation, U-shaped correlation, positive correlation, and spurious correlation.

Finally, the third type of study examines potential relationships between social disclosure and economic performance. The hypothesis is that (a) social disclosure reduces investors' information uncertainty and (b) social disclosures are correlated (positively and negatively) with economic performance. The first hypothesis examines the relationship between social disclosure and economic performance based on market variables.[24,25] The second hypothesis examines the relationship between social disclosure and economic performance based on accounting variables.[26] The tested accounting-based economic performance variables include, in addition to those cited for the second type of studies, a measure based on a factor of analysis of forty-eight accounting ratios. The various market-based economic performance measures include (a) monthly return differences, (b) monthly average residuals, (c) monthly portfolio returns, and (d) standardized abnormal mean adjusted daily returns. Most of these studies control for other variables such as size, beta, year, industry, stock ownership distribution, or industry image. Again, as in the previous two types of studies, the results vary among a continuum from negative correlation to positive correlation and include one case of U-shaped correlation.

This review of these three types of studies points to three major inconsistencies: (a) a lack of theory, (b) diversity of empirical databases examined, and (c) the absence of a single conceptual framework to analyze the relationship between social disclosure, social performance, and economic performance. These inconsistencies contribute substantially to the diversity of study results. This chapter attempts to correct these limitations.

## FACTORS INFLUENCING THE DECISION TO DISCLOSE SOCIAL INFORMATION

### General Rationale

Research on the economic consequences of accounting choice seeks to explain firms' choices of accounting techniques and/or strategies. Using agency theory and other economic factors, these studies draw from analyses by Watts,[27] Jensen,[28] and Watts and Zimmerman.[29] These models attempt to link the choice of accounting techniques to contracting and monitoring costs, and political visibility. In general, it is hypothesized that firms facing higher contracting and monitoring costs are more likely to choose accounting methods that increase reported income, and firms with high political visibility are more likely to choose income-decreasing techniques.[30]

Specific and material expenditures are necessary to achieve social performance goals. The same expenditures reduce net income. While the image-building and public interest concerns may govern the decision to spend for social performance and to disclose social information, more practical considerations may also play a role. In particular, social performance can have a material effect on the current period's reported net

**Exhibit 6.1**
**Model of the Determinants of the Corporate Decision to Disclose Social Information**

+ Social performance

+ Economic performance

                                                    Social disclosure
+ Political visibility
  (size hypothesis)

− Contracting and monitoring costs
  (debt/equity hypothesis)

income and on key financial variables that are constrained by contractual agreements. Therefore, following the agency framework rationale, given that the decision to disclose social information follows a decrease in reported net income resulting from social performance outlays, this study hypothesizes that firms with lower contracting and monitoring costs, and having high political visibility, are more likely to disclose social information. In addition, given that the outlays for social performance assume adequate resources and therefore good economic performance, the decision to disclose social information is also positively correlated with the economic performance or profitability.

*Ceteris paribus*, this study hypothesizes that the decision to disclose social information is positively correlated with economic performance, economic performance, and political visibility, and negatively correlated with contracting and monitoring costs (see Exhibit 6.1). The proxy for contracting and monitoring costs includes leverage. Proxies for political visibility to be examined include size, capital intensity, and systematic risk. The proxy for social performance includes a reputational index that lists companies exhibiting especially good or bad social performance. The detailed rationale for the hypotheses are examined next.

### Social Performance

When a firm really engages in socially responsible types of activity involving the outlay of resources, it is done to create an impression of sensitivity to important nonmarket influences that may be in the long-term interest of the shareholders. Managers, naturally, are eager to reveal this concern to appropriate interest groups, the shareholders, and the public in general. One practical way to advertise this concern is through some form of social disclosure in the annual reports. Therefore, the following hypothesis is proposed:

$H_{o1}$:   Firms disclose social information in proportion to the perceived social performance ($H_1$).

Measuring social performance is difficult, however, because of its link to the issue of organizational effectiveness: "An organization's social performance is an indistinguishable component of its effectiveness."[31] Social performance is adequately defined as the extent to which an organization meets the needs, expectations, and demands of certain external constituencies beyond those directly linked to the company's products/markets. It is also referred to as participant observation, ecological model, or external effectiveness.[32-34] Its measurement, involving the perceptions of all external constituencies in an overall index, is at best impractical. One approach, however, is to develop *reputational indices*, listing companies exhibiting good or bad social performance. The one used in this study is based on a survey conducted by *Business and Society Review* among business people, in which forty-five leading corporations were rated in terms of social performance.

## Financial Variables

The restrictive covenants included in debt agreements are intended to reduce management's ability to create wealth transfers between shareholders and bondholders.[35,36] Common limitations include limits on financial leverage (long-term debt to total assets ratio) and limits on payout rates (dividends to a maximum available unrestricted retained earnings). The decision to disclose social information follows an outlay for social performance that reduces earnings. Therefore, the following hypothesis is proposed:

$H_{o2}$:   Firms that disclose social information are less financially levered ($H_2$), and have lower ratios of dividends to unrestricted earnings ($H_3$).

### Political Visibility

Politically visible firms are generally criticized by interest groups on the basis of their reported accounting numbers. Such firms can choose accounting techniques and actions that reduce their reported income and alter or reduce their political visibility. Politically visible firms are generally of larger size, have greater capital intensity, and have relatively high systematic market risk (betas). Given that the decision to disclose the social information follows an outlay for social performance that reduces earnings, incentives may exist for politically visible firms to engage in this form of disclosure.

Politically visible firms are also asked to respond to the demands of social activists. Various authors argue that many social disclosures are nothing but public relations gestures meant to ward off grass roots attacks by social activists (Fry and Hock, 1976).

Therefore, based on both arguments the following hypothesis is proposed:

$H_{o3}$: Firms that disclose social information tend to be larger ($H_4$), have higher capital intensive ratios ($H_5$), and have higher betas ($H_6$).

### Economic Performance

The relationship between social disclosure, social performance, and economic performance is best expressed by the view that social responsiveness requires from management the same superior skills required to make a firm profitable. As expressed by Alexander and Buchholz: "Socially aware and concerned management will also possess the requisite skills to run a superior company in the traditional sense of financial performance, thus making its firm an attractive investment."[37] Consequently, socially responsive firms in terms of social disclosure and social performance should outperform nonresponsive or less responsive ones in terms of profitability as measured by accounting variables like a rate of return on investment, and market variables like a differential stock price return. Therefore, the following hypothesis is proposed:

$H_{o4}$: Firms that disclose social information tend to have greater rates of return ($H_7$) and greater differential stock price returns ($H_8$).

If this hypothesis is rejected, it gives more credence to the opposing view that socially responsible firms will be at a competitive disadvantage owing to the added expense incurred by such behavior.[38]

## VARIABLE DEFINITIONS

As explained earlier, this study proposes a testable model that may explain the decision to disclose social information in terms of variables measuring social performance, monitoring and contracting costs, political visibility, and economic performance. The dependent and independent variables of the model are defined as follows:

1. The decision to disclose social information has been measured in various ways in the empirical studies investigating the relationships between either social disclosure and social performance or social disclosure and economic performance. The most popular and exhaustive measure used is based on a social disclosure scale derived from Ernst and Ernst surveys of social responsibility disclosure by the U.S. companies. It is used in this study in the form of the following scale: the number of social responsibility programs. The scale varies from 0 to 13. This scale will be used as the dependent variable expressing the decision to disclose and/or the extent of disclosure of social information.

2. Social performance is measured in several ways in the empirical studies cited in the related literature section. Given the difficulties of measuring social performance as organizational effectiveness, these studies generally rely on a reputational index such as that of forty-five leading companies' performance based on a survey conducted by *Business and Society Review* among business people. This study relies on the survey-based reputational scale, which yields a ranking of the firms' degree of social responsibility ranging from outstanding to poor.

3. Monitoring and contracting cost variables in this study include leverage, and dividends to unrestricted retained earnings. They are measured as follows:

a. leverage = total debt/total assets;
b. dividends to unrestricted retained earnings = dividends/unrestricted retained earnings.

The variable definitions are compatible with other positive empirical studies to ensure comparability of results.

4. Political visibility proxies in this study include size, capital intensity, and systematic risk. They are measured as follows:

   a. size = log of net sales;

   b. capital-intensive ratio = gross fixed assets/sales;

   c. systematic risk = beta coefficient derived from the market model for the period 1970–1974.

Again, the political visibility variables are compatible with other positive empirical studies ensuring comparability.

5. Economic performance in this study includes rate of return and stock price return. They are measured as follows:

   a. accounting return on assets = net income/total assets;

   b. stock price return = differentiated stock price for the five years 1970–1974.

## EMPIRICAL TESTS

### Model and Data

The various hypotheses and variables are combined into an empirically testable model specified as follows:

$$SOD = \alpha_0 + \alpha_1 SOP + \alpha_2 DR + \alpha_3 BETA + \alpha_4 LEV$$
$$+ \alpha_5 DIVUE + \alpha_6 NITA + \alpha_7 LSAL + \alpha_8 CI + e$$

where:

$SOD$ = social disclosure of the firm expressed by the number of social programs disclosed,

$SOP$ = social performance measured as a ranking of corporation by business executives,

$DR$ = stock price differential return,

$BETA$ = systematic market risk,

$LEV$ = total debt/total assets,

$DIVUE$ = dividends/retained earnings,

$NITA$ = net income/total assets,

**Exhibit 6.2**
**Sample of Companies Used in the Study**

| Company | Industry Code |
| --- | --- |
| IBM | 3680 |
| General Electric | 3600 |
| Ford Motor | 3711 |
| General Motors | 3711 |
| Mobil Oil | 2911 |
| Standard Oil of Indiana | 2911 |
| Chrysler | 3711 |
| RCA | 3651 |
| Westinghouse | 3600 |
| Exxon | 2911 |
| E. I. Du Pont | 2800 |
| Shell Oil | 2911 |
| Union Carbide | 2841 |
| International Telephone and Telegraph | 3661 |
| General Telephone and Electric | 4811 |
| Gulf Oil | 2911 |
| Bethlehem Steel | 3558 |
| Goodyear Tire and Rubber | 3000 |
| Standard Oil of California | 8911 |
| U.S. Steel | 2911 |
| LTV | 3310 |
| Texaco | 2911 |
| Esmark | 2010 |

$LSAL$ = log of net sales, and

$CI$ = capital intensity (gross fixed assets/sales).

Given this specification of the model, the sample includes firms for which information was first available for both $SOD$ (social disclosure) and $SOP$ (social performance). In other words, the companies had to be included in both the Ernst and Ernst social disclosure survey (Ernst and Ernst, 1973) and the survey conducted by *Business and Society Review*, ranking firms' social performance (''Industry Rates Itself,'' 1972). This procedure results in a sample of twenty-three corporations shown in Exhibit 6.2.

## Empirical Tests of the Model—Regression Results

Based on the model, a regression was run for the year 1973. Exhibit 6.3 contains the overall regression results. The model appears highly

**Exhibit 6.3**
**Regression Results**

| Variable Definition | Intercept | Social Performance | Return | Market Risk | Leverage | Dividend Payout | Profit-ability | Size | Capital Intensity | Model Significance | |
|---|---|---|---|---|---|---|---|---|---|---|---|
| Variable | $\alpha_0$ | SOP | DR | BETA | LEV | DIVUE | NITA | LSAL | CI | F | $R^2$ |
| Predicted Sign | | - | + | + | - | + | + | + | + | | |
| Coefficient 64.347 | 11.475 | -0.223 | 80.009 | 10.002 | -36.42 | 32.13 | -86.13 | 1.020 | -2.25 | 3.158 | |
| Standardised Estimate (43.97%) | 0 | -0.4643 | 0.1828 | 0.8505 | -1.295 | 0.3911 | -0.7480 | 0.4236 | -0.3079 | | |
| t-score | 1.748 | -2.342 | 0.846 | 2.763 | -2.705 | 1.396 | -1.718 | 1.997 | -1.424 | | |
| Significance | 0.1023 | 0.0345[a] | 0.4120 | 0.0153[a] | 0.0171[a] | 0.1844 | 0.1078 | 0.0657[b] | 0.1764 | 0.0289[b] | |

[a] significant at $\alpha = 0.05$.

[b] significant at $\alpha = 0.10$.

significant: $(F = 3.158, \alpha = 0.0289)$, $R^2 = 64.347$, and $R^2 = 43.79$ percent.

The regression coefficients for *SOP, BETA, LEV,* and *LSAL* are significant at the 0.10 level or less, and have the expected signs. In other words, the decision to disclose social information is found to be significantly associated with social performance (measured by *SOP*), financial monitoring and contracting costs (measured by *LEV*), and political visibility (measured by *LSAL* and *BETA*).

Interpretations of the regression results and the individual coefficients are contingent on the aptness of the model and are effected by the presence of multicollinearity. The remainder of this section discusses the results of the tests in each of these areas, a possible problem, and potential remedies.

The tested model appears to be well specified. Results from the various tests and plots suggested by Neter, Wasserman, and Kutner[39] provide evidence that the ordinary least squares (*OLS*) linear regression model is appropriate for the analysis. More specifically, statistical tests (Shapiro-Wilks *W* statistic test of normality) and plots (including stem and leaf, box, and normal probability graphs) of more residuals indicate a linear function and error term having constant variance, independence, and a normal distribution.

Exhibit 6.4 results indicate the presence of multicollinearity. There are ten pairwise correlations of independent variables that are significant at the $p = 0.05$ level. This can adversely affect the interpretation of regression coefficients. When independent variables provide redundant information relative to the dependent variable, the individual coefficient's significance levels are usually underestimated. In some cases the sign of the coefficient is reversed versus the zero-order relationship. There is no agreement on what constitutes a high level of multicollinearity.

The method applied by Daley and Vigeland[40] is to calculate the coefficient multiple correlation, $R^2$, between each variable and all the others. The rule of thumb for serious multicollinearity is a multiple correlation coefficient greater than 80 percent. Exhibit 6.4 shows only one such value, the 82.94 percent for the variable *LEV* (leverage), which has significant pairwise correlations with both *BETA* (systematic risk) and *NITA* (net income/total assets) at 0.75469 and −0.7710, respectively. Thus the presence of these three variables in the model makes the interpretation of each of their regression coefficients potentially misleading. While there is no cure for multiple collinearity, there are several feasible remedies that can help clarify statistical relationships among the model variables.

**Exhibit 6.4**
**Correlation between Variables**

| | | | | | Pairwise | | | |
|---|---|---|---|---|---|---|---|---|
| Variables | *SOP* | *DR* | *BETA* | *LEV* | *DIVUE* | *NITA* | *LSAL* | *CI* |
| *SOP* | 1.000 | | | | | | | |
| DR | 0.2248 | 1.000 | | | | | | |
| BETA | 0.2172 | −0.1528 | 1.000 | | | | | |
| LEV | 0.1558 | −0.1905 | 0.75469[a] | 1.000 | | | | |
| DIVUE | −0.4284[b] | −0.1637 | −0.5066[a] | −0.3479[b] | 1.000 | | | |
| NITA | −0.3558 | 0.1823 | −0.6288[a] | −0.7710[a] | 0.5273[a] | 1.000 | | |
| LSAL | −0.4597[b] | 0.2427 | −0.4683 | −0.2772 | 0.4116[b] | 0.4877[a] | 1.000 | |
| CI | 0.1780 | 0.3271 | −0.1878 | −0.2529 | 0.2428 | 0.0962 | 0.1098 | 1.000 |
| (Dependent) SOD | −0.5538[a] | −0.1039 | −0.0363 | −0.3032 | 0.2888 | 0.4167[b] | 0.4334[b] | −0.19086 |
| Multiple $R^2$% | 22.34 | 21.68 | 69.50 | 82.94 | 51.08 | 65.65 | 13.18 | 43.07 |

[a] Significant at $\alpha = 0.01$.

[b] Significant at $\alpha = 0.05$.

$R^2$, coefficient of multiple determination between variable $i$ and all independent variables.

One approach is to delete variables, thereby directly eliminating the source of the multicollinearity. Exhibit 6.4 reports the zero-order correlations between the dependent variable SOD (number of social programs disclosed) and each independent variable; the coefficients are significant at the level of $p = 0.05$ for SOP, NITA, and LSAL. Also run are regressions of various combinations of independent variables with SOD. The purpose was to examine the stability of the regression coefficient values as each of the three related variables (LEV, BETA, and NITA) are removed from the model. Only NITA's sign changes; removing LEV creates a positive regression coefficient for NITA. In each case the overall model's explanatory power is reduced and the model may not be as well specified.

Another approach is to use a different statistical method, such as maximum likelihood (ML) estimation-based ridge regression (LISREL). Adopting these methods (with their substantial complexities relative to OLS) is not warranted for this analysis because the residuals are normally distributed, so the ML estimators are identical to those of least squares regression.[41]

In summary, the model is well specified and the effects of multicollinearity do not appear serious overall. The fact that some or all independent variables are correlated among themselves does not, in general, inhibit our ability to obtain a good fit nor does it tend to affect inferences about mean responses or predictions of new observations, provided these inferences are made within the region of observations. The major effect of multicollinearity appears to be an unstable estimate of the NITA regression coefficient when LEV is also in the model. This statistical phenomenon may partially explain why previous empirical studies report such varying relationships between social disclosure (SOD) and economic performance (NITA). Otherwise the reported model is well specified and its regressed coefficients stable. Deleting variables, such as LEV, to reduce multicollinearity reduces the model's explanatory power and may lead to specification errors.

## DISCUSSION

This chapter proposes a positive model of the decision to disclose social information in terms of social performance, economic performance, financial performance, and political visibility. The results verify the significant importance of (a) social performance as measured by an organizational effectiveness index, (b) financial performance as measured by leverage, and (c) political visibility as measured by size and systematic risk. These results raise fundamental issues and concerns for social responsibility accounting.

First, the significant and positive association of social disclosure with social performance shows that social improvements by a firm are quickly capitalized by social disclosure in an attempt to create an impression of sensitivity to important nonmarket influences that may be in the long-term interest of the shareholders. It is interesting to note that those studies finding no correlation or negative correlation between social performance and social disclosure rely on either student ratings or on the CEP pollution performance index. Both indices do not, however, measure social performance per se, but rather perceived social performance by individuals who cannot be considered constituents, or pollution control records that do not represent overall effectiveness. Future research should concentrate on the development of representative measures of overall effectiveness.

Second, the significant and positive association of social disclosure with political visibility as measured by size and systematic risk points to the tendency of managers to choose an accounting procedure to reduce reported earnings and political costs. This phenomenon is known as the size hypothesis. It assumes that large firms are more politically sensitive than small firms and face differential incentives in their choice of accounting procedures that lead them to defer reported earnings from current to future periods. In the context of this study the size hypothesis is verified in the sense that the larger the firm, the more likely it is that the managers authorize outlays for social performance that defer reported earnings from current to future periods. This is consistent with other findings supporting the size hypothesis in the choice of accounting procedures.

Third, the significant negative association of social disclosure with financial leverage points to the tendency of managers with high debt/equity ratios to choose an accounting procedure that reduces reported earnings. This phenomenon is known as the debt/equity hypothesis. It assumes that the larger a firm's debt/equity ratio, the more likely the firm's manager is to select accounting procedures that shift reported earnings from future periods to the current period. In the context of this study, and because of the negative sign of leverage, the size hypothesis is also verified in the sense that the larger the debt/equity ratio of a firm, the more likely it is that a manager is going to authorize outlays for social performance that defer reported earnings from current to future periods. This is consistent with other findings supporting the debt/equity hypothesis in the choice of accounting procedures.

Fourth, the insignificant and negative regression coefficient yet positive pairwise correlation association of economic performance with social disclosure is attributed to the multicollinearity problem encountered in the study. This multicollinearity affect may also explain the observance in other studies of either positive, negative, or no correlation of probability with social disclosure.

## LIMITATIONS

Various limitations point to the need for more research on the determinants of the decision to disclose social information and replication of this study under new conditions.

First, the choice of the year 1973 was made for two reasons: (a) both social disclosure measures from the Ernst and Ernst publications and social performance measures for the businessmen rankings are available for that period, and (b) most studies investigating the issue of the association between social disclosure and economic performance relied on the same measures and the same period providing us with the opportunity to compare our results with their findings and to show the superiority of a model of social disclosure that includes as determinants: social performance, economic performance, political costs, and financial performance. Needless to say, this study should be replicated to test the model in other periods, using different measures of social disclosure and social performance.

Second, this study relied on a reputational scale as a measure of social performance. Studies relying on reputational scales differ in their level of refinement and yield conflicting results. In addition, the concept of corporate social performance is best limited to the concept of organizational effectiveness. A measurement of social performance in the context of effectiveness calls for (a) a better identification of the firm's external constituents, (b) a measurement of constituent satisfaction, and (c) development of an overall index encompassing these different criteria so that firms can be ranked in terms of their overall social performance.

Third, because of the data constraints on the dependent and independent variables, our sample is homogeneous including companies with a rather high political visibility. Replication of this study using less politically visible companies and those that are more service-oriented is warranted.

## CONCLUSIONS

This study develops and empirically investigates a positive model of the decision to disclose social information in terms of social performance, economic performance, financial performance, and political visibility. Based on 1973 data, when measures in all the variables were available, the results suggested that when social performance is measured by business executive rankings, the firms that disclose social information, in terms of the number of categories of social disclosure disclosed in the annual report, appear to be (a) those perceived to display social responsiveness, (b) those having higher systematic risk and lower leverage, and (c) those that were larger in size.

This research relied on the Ernst and Ernst data for a measure of social disclosure and a reputational index for a measure of social performance. More evidence is needed based on other periods and other countries' measures of social disclosure and social performance before any generalizations can be made.

## NOTES

1. This chapter has been adapted from Ahmed Belkaoui and P. G. Karpik, "Determinants of the Corporate Decision to Disclose Social Information," *Accounting, Auditing and Accountability Journal* 2, no. 1 (1989), pp. 36–51. Reprinted with permission from MCB University Press.

2. R. J. Aldag and K. M. Bartol, "Empirical Studies of Corporate Social Performance and Policy: A Survey of Problems and Results," in L. E. Preston, ed., *Research in Corporate Social Performance and Policy*, Vol. 1 (Greenwich, Conn.: JAI Press, 1978), pp. 165–199.

3. M. Epstein, E. Flamholtz, and J. J. McDonough, "Corporate Social Accounting in the United States of America: State of the Arts and Future Prospects," *Accounting, Organizations and Society* 2 (1976), pp. 23–42.

4. L. E. Preston, "Book Review: Teaching Materials in Business and Society," *California Management Review* 4 (Spring 1983), pp. 158–173.

5. A. Belkaoui, *Socio-Economic Accounting* (Westport, Conn.: Greenwood Press, 1984).

6. A. A. Ullmann, "Data in Search of a Theory: A Critical Examination of the Relationships among Social Performance, Social Disclosure, and Economic Performance of U.S. Firms," *Academy of Management Review* 10 (1985), pp. 540–557.

7. W. F. Abbott and R. J. Monsen, "On the Measurement of Corporate Social Responsibility: Self-Reported Disclosure as a Method of Measuring Cor-

porate Social Involvement,'' *Academy of Management Journal* 22 (1979), pp. 501–515.

8. E. H. Bowman and M. Haire, ''A Strategic Posture toward Corporate Social Responsibility,'' *California Management Review* 18, no. 2 (1975), pp. 49–58.

9. M. Freedman and B. Jaggi, ''Pollution Disclosures, Pollution Performance and Economic Performance,'' *Omega*, 10 (1982), pp. 167–176.

10. F. Fry and R. J. Hock, ''Who Claims Corporate Responsibility? The Biggest and the Worst,'' *Business and Society Review/Innovation* 18 (1976), pp. 62–65.

11. R. W. Ingram and K. B. Frazier, ''Environmental Performance and Corporate Disclosure,'' *Journal of Accounting Research* 18 (1980), pp. 614–622.

12. L. E. Preston, ''Analyzing Corporate Social Performance: Methods and Results,'' *Journal of Contemporary Business* 7 (1978), pp. 135–150.

13. J. Wiseman, ''An Evaluation of Environmental Disclosures Made in Corporate Annual Reports,'' *Accounting, Organizations and Society* 7 (1982), pp. 53–63.

14. Ernst and Ernst, *Social Responsibility Disclosure, 1973 Survey* (Cleveland, Ohio: Ernst and Ernst, 1973).

15. ''How Business School Students Rate Corporations,'' *Business and Society Review*, 2 (1972), pp. 20–21.

16. ''Industry Rates Itself,'' *Business and Society Review* 1 (1972), pp. 96–99.

17. M. R. Moskowitz, ''Choosing Socially Responsible Stocks,'' *Business and Society Review* 1 (1972), pp. 29–42.

18. G. J. Alexander and R. A. Buchholz, ''Corporate Social Responsibility and Stock Market Performance,'' *Academy of Management Journal* 21 (1978), pp. 479–486.

19. J. H. Bragdon and J. A. T. Marlin, ''Is Pollution Profitable?'' *Risk Management* 19, no. 4 (1972), pp. 9–18.

20. K. H. Chen and R. W. Metcalf, ''The Relationship between Pollution Control Record and Financial Indicators Revisited,'' *The Accounting Review* 55 (1980), pp. 168–177.

21. P. L. Cochran and R. A. Wood, ''Corporate Social Responsibility and Financial Performance,'' *Academy of Management Journal* 27 (1984), pp. 42–56.

22. H. R. Folger and F. Nutt, ''A Note on Social Responsibility and Stock Valuation,'' *Academy of Management Journal* 18 (1975), pp. 155–160.

23. B. L. Kedia and E. C. Kuntz, ''The Contest of Social Performance: An Empirical Study of Texas Banks,'' in L. E. Preston, *Research in Corporate Social Performance and Policy*, Vol. III (Greenwich, Conn.: JAI Press, 1981), pp. 133–154.

24. A. Belkaoui, "The Impact of the Disclosure of the Environmental Effects of Organizational Behavior on the Market," *Financial Management* 5, no. 4 (1976), pp. 26–31.

25. B. Jaggi and M. Freedman, "An Analysis of the Impact of Corporate Pollution Disclosures Included in Annual Financial Statements on Investors' Decisions," *Advances in Public Interest Accounting* (in press).

26. R. W. Ingram and K. B. Frazier, "Narrative Disclosures and Annual Reports," *Journal of Business Research* 11 (1983), pp. 49–60.

27. R. Watts, "Corporate Financial Statements: Product of Market and Political Processes," *Australian Journal of Management* (April 1977), pp. 52–75.

28. M. C. Jensen, "Reflections on the State of Accounting Research and the Regulation of Accounting," *Stanford Lectures in Accounting* (Stanford, Calif.: Stanford University, 1976).

29. R. Watts and J. Zimmerman, *Positive Accounting Theory* (Englewood Cliffs, N.J.: Prentice-Hall, 1986).

30. R. Holthausen and R. Leftwich, "The Economic Consequences of Accounting Choice: Implications of Costly Contracting and Monitoring," *Journal of Accounting and Economics* 5 (1983), pp. 75–117.

31. R. Strand, "A Systems Paradigm of Organizational Adaptations to the Social Environment," *Academy of Management Review* 8 (1983), p. 90.

32. M. A. Keeley, "Social Justice Approach to Organizational Evaluation," *Administrative Quality* 23 (1978), pp. 272–292.

33. R. H. Kilman and R. P. Herden, "Towards a Systematic Methodology for Evaluating the Impact of Interviews on Organizational Effectiveness," *Academy of Management Review*, 1, no. 3 (1976), pp. 87–88.

34. R. H. Miles, *Macro-Organizational Behavior* (Glenview, Ill.: Scott-Foresman, 1980).

35. M. C. Jensen and W. Meckling, "Theory of the Firm: Managerial Behavior, Agency Costs and Ownership Structure," *Journal of Financial Economics* 3 (1976), pp. 305–360.

36. C. Smith and J. Warner, "Financial Contracting: An Analysis of Bond Covenants," *Journal of Financial Economics* 7 (1979), pp. 117–162.

37. G. J. Alexander and R. A. Buchholz, "Corporate Social Responsibility and Stock Market Performance," *Academy of Managerial Journal* 21 (1978), p. 479.

38. S. C. Vance, "Are Socially Responsible Corporations Good Investment Risks?" *Management Review* 64, no. 8 (1975), pp. 19–24.

39. N. Neter, W. Wasserman, and M. H. Kutner, *Applied Linear Statistical Models*, 2nd ed. (Homewood, Ill.: Richard D. Irwin, 1985).

40. L. A. Daley and R. L. Vigeland, "The Effects of Debt Convenants and Political Costs on the Choice of Accounting Methods: The Case of Accounting for R&D Costs," *Journal of Accounting and Economics* (December 1983), pp. 195–212.

41. Elazar J. Pedhazur, *Multiple Regression in Behavioral Research*, 2nd ed. (New York: Holt, Rinehart and Winston, 1982), p. 639.

## SELECTED READINGS

Abbott, W. F., and Monsen, R. J. "On the Measurement of Corporate Social Responsibility: Self-Reported Disclosure as a Method of Measuring Corporate Social Involvement." *Academy of Management Journal* 22 (1979), pp. 501–515.

Aldag, R. J., and Bartol, K. M. "Empirical Studies of Corporate Social Performance and Policy: A Survey of Problems and Results." In L. E. Preston, ed., *Research in Corporate Social Performance and Policy*, Vol. 1. Greenwich, Conn.: JAI Press, 1978: pp. 165–99.

Alexander, G. J., and Buchholz, R. A. "Corporate Social Responsibility and Stock Market Performance." *Academy of Management Journal* 21 (1978), pp. 479–486.

Anderson, J. C., and Frankle, A. W. "Voluntary Social Reporting: An Iso-Beta Portfolio Analysis." *The Accounting Review* 55 (1980), pp. 468–479.

Belkaoui, A. "The Impact of the Disclosure of the Environmental Effects of Organizational Behavior on the Market." *Financial Management* 5, no. 4 (1976), pp. 26–31.

———. *Socio-Economic Accounting*. Westport, Conn.: Greenwood Press, 1984.

Bowen, R., Noreen, E., and Lacey, J. "Determinants of the Corporate Decision to Capitalize Interest." *Journal of Accounting and Economics* 3 (1981), pp. 151–179.

Bowman, E. H. "Strategy, Annual Reports, and Alchemy." *California Management Review* 20, no. 3 (1978), pp. 64–71.

Bowman, E. H., and Haire, M. "A Strategic Posture toward Corporate Social Responsibility." *California Management Review* 18, no. 2 (1975), pp. 49–58.

Bragdon, J. H., and Marlin, J. A. T. "Is Pollution Profitable?" *Risk Management* 19, no. 4 (1972), pp. 9–18.

Chen, K. H., and Metcalf, R. W. "The Relationship between Pollution Control Record and Financial Indicators Revisited." *The Accounting Review* 55 (1980), pp. 168–177.

Cochran, P. L., and Wood, R. A. "Corporate Social Responsibility and Financial Performance." *Academy of Management Journal* 27 (1984), pp. 42–56.

Cowen, S. S., Ferreri, L. B., and Parker, L. D. "The Impact of Corporate Characteristics on Social Responsibility Disclosure: A Typology and Frequency-Based Analysis." *Accounting, Organizations and Society* (March 1987), pp. 111–122.

Daley, L. A., and Vigeland, R. L. "The Effects of Debt Covenants and Political Costs on the Choice of Accounting Methods: The Case of Accounting for R&D Costs." *Journal of Accounting and Economics* (December 1983), pp. 195–212.

Deakin, E. B. "An Analysis of Differences between Non-Major Oil Firms Using Successful Efforts and Full Cost Methods." *The Accounting Review* (October 1979), pp. 722–734.

Dhaliwal, D. "The Effect of the Firm's Capital Structure on the Choice of Accounting Network." *The Accounting Review* 50 (1980), pp. 78–84.

Dhaliwal, D., Salamon, G., and Smith, E. "The Effect of Owner versus Management Control on the Choice of Accounting Methods." *Journal of Accounting and Economics* 4 (July 1982), pp. 41–53.

Epstein, M., Flamholtz, E., and McDonough, J. J. "Corporate Social Accounting in the United States of America: State of the Arts and Future Prospects." *Accounting, Organizations and Society* 5 (1976), pp. 23–42.

Ernst and Ernst. *Social Responsibility Disclosure, 1973 Survey.* Cleveland, Ohio: Ernst and Ernst, 1973.

Folger, H. R., and Nutt, F. "A Note on Social Responsibility and Stock Valuation." *Academy of Management Journal* 18 (1975), pp. 155–160.

Freedman, M., and Jaggi, B. "Pollution Disclosures, Pollution Performance and Economic Performance." *Omega* 10 (1982), pp. 167–176.

Fry, F., and Hock, R. J. "Who Claims Corporate Responsibility? The Biggest and the Worst." *Business and Society Review/Innovation* 18 (1976), pp. 62–65.

Gray, R., Owen, D., and Maunders, K. "Corporate Social Reporting: Emerging Trends in Accountability and the Social Contract." *Accounting, Auditing and Accountability* 1, no. 1 (1988), pp. 6–20.

Hagerman, R., and Zmijewski, M. "Some Economic Determinants of Accounting Policy." *Journal of Accounting and Economics* 1 (1979), pp. 142–161.

Holthausen, R., and Leftwich, R. "The Economic Consequences of Accounting Choice: Implications of Costly Contracting and Monitoring." *Journal of Accounting and Economics* 5 (1983), pp. 75–117.

"How Business School Students Rate Corporations." *Business and Society Review* 2 (1972), pp. 20–21.

"Industry Rates Itself." *Business and Society Review* 1 (1972), pp. 96–99.

Ingram, R. W. "An Investigation of the Information Content of (Certain) Social Responsibility Disclosures." *Journal of Accounting Research* 18 (1980), pp. 614–622.

Ingram, R. W., and Frazier, K. B. "Environmental Performance and Corporate Disclosure." *Journal of Accounting Research* 18 (1980), pp. 614–622.

———. "Narrative Disclosures and Annual Reports." *Journal of Business Research* 11 (1983), pp. 49–60.

Jaggi, B., and Freedman, M. "An Analysis of the Impact of Corporate Pollution Disclosures Included in Annual Financial Statements on Investors' Decisions." *Advances in Public Interest Accounting* (in press).

Jensen, M. C. "Reflections on the State of Accounting Research and the Regulation of Accounting." *Stanford Lectures in Accounting*. Stanford, Calif.: Stanford University, 1976.

Jensen, M. C., and Meckling, W. "Theory of the Firm: Managerial Behavior, Agency Costs and Ownership Structure." *Journal of Financial Economics* 3 (1976), pp. 305–360.

Judge, G. G., et al. *The Theory and Practice of Econometrics*. New York: Wiley, 1980.

Kedia, B. L., and Kuntz, E. C. "The Contest of Social Performance: An Empirical Study of Texas Banks." In L. E. Preston, ed., *Research in Corporate Social Performance and Policy*, Vol. III. Greenwich, Conn.: JAI Press, 1981: pp. 135–154.

Keeley, M. A. "Social Justice Approach to Organizational Evaluation." *Administrative Quality* 23 (1978), pp. 272–292.

Kilman, R. H., and Herden, R. P. "Towards a Systematic Methodology for Evaluating the Impact of Interviews on Organizational Effectiveness." *Academy of Management Review* 1, no. 3 (1976), pp. 87–88.

Lilien, S., and Pastena, V. "Determinants of Intramethod Choice in the Oil and Gas Industry." *Journal of Accounting and Economics* (December 1982), pp. 145–170.

Miles, R. H. *Macro-Organizational Behavior*. Glenview, Ill.: Scott Foresman, 1980.

Moskowitz, M. R. "Choosing Socially Responsible Stocks." *Business and Society Review* 1 (1972), pp. 29–42.

Neter, N., Wasserman, W., and Kutner, M. H. *Applied Linear Statistical Models*, 2nd ed. Homewood, Ill.: Richard D. Irwin, 1985.

Parket, L. R., and Eibirt, H. "Socially Responsible: The Underlying Factors." *Business Horizons* 18, no. 4 (1975), pp. 5–10.

Pedhazur, Elazar J. *Multiple Regression in Behavioral Research*, 2nd ed. New York: Holt, Rinehart and Winston, 1982.

Preston, L. E. "Analyzing Corporate Social Performance: Methods and Results." *Journal of Contemporary Business* 7 (1978), pp. 135–150.

———. "Book Review: Teaching Materials in Business and Society." *California Management Review* (Spring 1983), pp. 158–173.

Shane, P. B., and Spicer, B. H. "Market Response to Environmental Information Produced Outside the Firm." *The Accounting Review* 58 (1983), pp. 521–538.

Smith, C., and Warner, J. "Financial Contracting: An Analysis of Bond Covenants." *Journal of Financial Economics* 7 (1979), pp. 117–162.

Spicer, B. H. "Investors, Corporate Social Performance and Information Disclosure: An Empirical Study." *The Accounting Review* 53 (1978), pp. 94–111.

————. "Market Risk, Accounting Data and Companies' Pollution Control Records." *Journal of Business Finance and Accounting* 5 (1978), pp. 67–83.

Strand, R. "A Systems Paradigm of Organizational Adaptations to the Social Environment." *Academy of Management Review* 8 (1983), p. 90.

Trotman, K. T., and Bradley, G. W. "Association between Social Responsibility Disclosure and Characteristics of Companies." *Accounting, Organizations and Society* (December 1981), pp. 355–362.

Ullmann, A. A. "Data in Search of a Theory: A Critical Examination of the Relationships among Social Performance, Social Disclosure, and Economic Performance of U.S. Firms." *Academy of Management Review* 10 (1985), pp. 540–557.

Vance, S. C. "Are Socially Responsible Corporations Good Investment Risks?" *Management Review* 64, no. 8 (1975), pp. 19–24.

Watts, R. "Corporate Financial Statements: Product of Market and Political Processes." *Australian Journal of Management* (April 1977), pp. 52–75.

Watts, R., and Zimmerman, J. *Positive Accounting Theory*. Englewood Cliffs, N.J.: Prentice-Hall, 1986.

————. "Towards a Positive Theory of the Determination of Accounting Standards." *The Accounting Review* 53 (1978), pp. 112–134.

Wiseman, J. "An Evaluation of Environmental Disclosures Made in Corporate Annual Reports." *Accounting, Organizations and Society* 7 (1982), pp. 53–63.

Zmijewski, M. E., and Hagerman, R. L. "An Income Strategy Approach to the Positive Theory of Accounting Standard Setting/Choice." *Journal of Accounting and Economics* 3 (1981), pp. 129–149.

# 7

# Financial Outcomes of Socio-Economic Accounting: The User Reaction to the Disclosure of Socio-Economic Accounting Information

## INTRODUCTION[1]

Conventional accounting data may be considered to be biased in favor of not putting ecology improvement programs into effect.[2] A major consequence, summed up by the Beams-Fertig thesis,[3] is that the corporations that report the least activity in avoiding social cost will appear more successful to investors and will be favored by the market. While empirical evidence on the above thesis is still inconclusive,[4-6] there is wide evidence that most external parties are increasingly demanding information on the environmental effects of organizational behavior.[7,8]

In response to this new situation the Study Group on Objectives of Financial Statements[9] proposed as an objective of financial statements the reporting of those activities that are important to the role of the enterprise in its social environment. In fact, most accounting associations have expressed a strong interest in the related issue of socio-economic accounting.[10] The resulting socio-economic accounting statements will differ from the conventional ones mainly through the internalization and disclosure of the social costs and benefits arising from production.[11] Strong evidence suggests that the socio-economic accounting type of information in the annual reports is significant and increasing.[12,13] Given this situation, the scholarly socio-economic accounting inquiry should focus on the development and validation of appropriate ways of measuring and disclosing social costs and benefits. Second, to assess the relevance of this new information to users it should also focus on evaluating the behavioral impact of such disclosure.

Accordingly, the purpose of this chapter is to report on a field experiment undertaken to determine whether the investment decision by an external user would be different with the addition of socio-economic accounting information. More specially, the following questions will be investigated:

1. Will the socio-economic accounting information cause the investment decision to be different from the conventional accounting information?

2. Assuming that investors are members of different professional groups, will the investment decision differ among those groups?

3. Assuming that the investment strategies of the investors are different, will it have any effect on the investment decision?

4. Finally, what are the demographic and perceptual variables most associated with these differential investment decisions when socio-economic accounting information is reported?

Similar questions have been the subject of studies investigating the decision effects resulting from using alternative accounting procedures. Most of the experiments used for those studies lack a theoretical framework to justify or motivate the reporting effects on individual decision making.[14] The research questions in this study, however, are theoretically supported by the linguistic relativity paradigm in accounting.[15-17]

The remainder of this chapter is divided into six sections. The next section relates this chapter to previous research on similar issues and questions. The second section introduces the linguistic relativity paradigm to motivate the research questions of interest in this study. The third section describes the experiment. The fourth section presents the results. The fifth section provides a discussion of the statistical results. The last section contains a brief summary and final conclusions.

## RELATED RESEARCH

The interest in this chapter lies in the behavior of users of accounting information for decision making. It adds more evidence to those studies that support the contention that alternative reporting procedures can influence decision making. These studies, which are mostly experiments, examined the decision effects resulting from using various alternative accounting procedures, namely:

a. using alternative inventory techniques;

b. using alternative methods of reporting income from intercorporate investments;

c. including segmented data in financial statements of diversified firms;

d. including additional information provided by a human resource accounting system;

e. including nonaccounting data;[18] and

f. using alternative tax allocation techniques.

From these studies it appears that the influence of alternative techniques on decision making has not always been conclusive. The degree of influence was found to depend on the nature of the particular decision defined by the experimental task, the nature and the characteristics of the decision makers used as subjects, and the content and format of the alternative accounting techniques presented in the experiment.

## THEORY

Accounting is language, and according to the Sapir-Whorf hypothesis, its lexical characteristics and grammatical rules will affect the linguistic and nonlinguistic behavior of users. On that basis Belkaoui[19] introduced four propositions derived from the linguistic relativity paradigm to conceptually integrate research findings on the impact of accounting rules and nonlinguistic behavior. Of particular interest to this study is the fourth hypothesis on the relationships between the accounting rules and nonlinguistic behavior.

In the context of the present study this proposition implies that, in general, the investment decision effects of investors from different professional groups using alternative forms of social and accounting information will be different.

## Hypothesis 1

In connection with Question (1), Hypothesis 1 was formulated:

$H_1$:    Socio-economic accounting information will induce different
         stock investment decision behavior than will conventional ac-
         counting information.

Since there is evidence to suggest some degree of association between
a firm's investment in social programs and its profitability, it may be
expected that investors will invest different amounts of funds in a firm
whose financial statements show an increase in "social awareness expenditures" as opposed to a firm showing a decrease or zero of these
expenditures. More importantly, on the basis of the proposition from the
linguistic relativity paradigm it may also be stated that the investment
decision as a nonlinguistic or managerial behavior will be facilitated or
rendered more difficult and consequently be different by the addition of
socio-economic accounting information.

Determining how different the investment decision is with the addition of socio-economic accounting information may be difficult. One
school of thought, mentioned earlier as the Beams-Fertig thesis, suggests
that the investors will favor firms showing a decrease in or zero "social awareness" expenditures. Another school of thought believes that
"ethical investors" form a clientele that responds to demonstrations of
corporate social concern or that corporate expenditures for social
improvement may benefit the corporation over the long run in many
ways.

## Hypothesis 2

In connection with Question (2), Hypothesis 2 was formulated:

$H_2$:    Given a reporting of either socio-economic or conventional
         accounting information, the investment decision will differ
         between different occupational groups.

While the main proposition from the linguistic relativity paradigm and
the first hypothesis suggest that the investment decision will differ with
the addition of socio-economic accounting information, it may be expected that this difference will be more evident for investors from dif-

ferent professional groups. The assumption is that occupational groups in the field of management differ in the extent of their exposure and orientation to accounting, which may lead their respective members to have a different understanding of, and pay differing levels of attention to, the socio-economic accounting information. In other words, for the accounting techniques to facilitate or render more difficult nonlinguistic or managerial behavior depends on the mastery of the difference between accounting techniques by the users and their membership to a given occupational group.

## Hypothesis 3

In connection with Question (3), Hypothesis 3 was formulated:

$H_3$: Given a reporting of either socio-economic or conventional accounting information, the investment decision will differ according to the type of investment strategy adopted.

Since there is evidence to suggest the existence of differences in investment style and strategy,[20] it may be assumed that they may lead eventually to different investment decisions. Combined with the linguistic relativity paradigm it may be suggested that the type of investment strategy adopted leads to a different understanding and attention paid to accounting information that will affect the investment decision. More detailed questions arising from the interaction effects are: (a) Will the difference in the investment behavior caused by the differences in the investment strategy be greater with the socio-economic than with the conventional accounting information? (b) Will the same difference in the investment behavior be a function of the occupational grouping?

## Hypothesis 4

In connection wilt Question (4), Hypothesis 4 was formulated:

$H_4$: Given either a reporting of socio-economic or conventional accounting information, the investment decision will be associated with perceptual and background variables.

Evidence from surveys and from laboratory experiments seems to indicate that investment behavior is a function of personal circumstances as expressed by demographic and perceptual variables. Again, combined with the linguistic relativity paradigm it may be suggested that the managerial behavior induced by the accounting techniques is associated with perceptual and background variables. More explicitly, the ecological concern and cognitive "makeup" of an individual may predispose him to understand and appreciate the socio-economic accounting disclosure and invest in socially responsible firms.

## METHOD

The experiment was designed as $3 \times 3 \times 2 \times N$ with the investment decision between two hypothetical firms as the only dependent variable. Two hundred and twenty-five subjects participated in the experiment.

### The Experiment Factors

Three independent variables were used: membership in professional groups, accounting information and investment strategy.

### Membership in Professional Groups

The subjects chosen belonged to three different occupational groups. They were (1) fourth-year undergraduate students majoring in accounting and finance, and first- and second-year M.B.A. students from the School of Commerce at Syracuse University, (2) senior officers from four Syracuse commercial banks, and (3) accountants, members of the National Association of Accountants (NAA), Syracuse chapter. In the choice of the three groups the main concern was to deal with the two caveats of behavior field experiment, namely the response ratio and validity. Following advice given by Barrett,[21] the response ratio was improved by employing the "captive audiences" of the local chapter of the NAA and the trust officers of local banks, and the validity problem was reduced by having the experiment run under the auspices of management at the subject's place of employment. The selection procedure consisted of first contacting the banks' upper management, and second, the NAA local chapter official and asking for cooperation. Seventy-five senior bank officers accepted participation in the experiment. Informed of the number of senior bank officers the NAA chapter secured the participation of 75 of their members. Finally 75 students were asked to participate in the experiment during class time. It is unlikely that the first 75 individuals contacted in the banking and accounting groups accepted participation in the experiment although the impression given was that the maximum number of senior officers had been secured in the banking group.

A liaison man for each bank and the NAA local chapter official were given the number of questionnaires required, given appropriate instructions, and given the responsibility of conducting the experiment.

## The Accounting Information Factor

This centered on the dichotomy between conventional and socio-economic accounting information. A problem arose in a proper definition of the socio-economic accounting information. Because of the variety of information susceptible to connote social responsibility[22] a choice was made for the disclosure of pollution abatement cost. The rationale for this choice is based upon (a) the general public belief that pollution abatement is a major indicator of a socially responsible firm[23] and (b) the relative materiality of these expenditures. For some large firms they may reach up to 4 percent of sales and 100 percent of capital investment (AAA, 1973, p. 88). They are also reported to be as high as 75 percent of capital investment in the steel industry.[24] Three accounting treatments were investigated: (1) the conventional treatment, not including any information on abatement costs, (2) a footnote treatment, including abating cost information in the footnotes, and (3) a total treatment, including the abatement cost information in both the profit-and-loss statement and the footnotes. The differentiation between the footnote treatment and the total treatment was based on the general stipulation that detailed information may be more useful than aggregated data.

## The Investment Strategy

This variable was operationalized by choosing two categories of investment style: (1) investment for dividend income and (2) investment for capital gains. The choice was limited to these two strategies thought to represent the extremes on a continuum of investment strategies. For example, Lewellen, Lease, and Schlarbaum[25] identified four objectives, namely, short-term capital gains, intermediate-term capital gains, long-term capital gains, and dividend income. Omitting the temporal distinction for capital gains the categories may be reduced to the two levels of the investment strategy factor chosen for this study.

### The Experimental Treatments and the Criterion Variable

In the experiment, the participants were asked to compare two firms, Abel Chemical Inc. and Jabel Chemical Inc., and then allocate a given amount of money as equity investment between the two firms. The 1971 annual report of an actual chemical company was chosen as a basis for the construction of financial statements in conformity with the three treatments of socio-economic accounting information. It is a chemical company that manufactures and markets organic and inorganic chemicals for textile, pulp, and paper agriculture markets, aerosol insecticides, chemical products, and mechanical components used in the air-conditioning and refrigeration industries. The two companies presented as Abel Chemical Inc. and Jabel Chemical Inc. were established through a modification of the financial characteristics of the chemical company initially selected. As a result the two firms are comparable in size but differ in terms of profitability. The manipulation of the experimental treatments resulted in three packets as follows:

1. The first packet includes the financial statements of both companies prepared according to conventional accounting treatments, i.e., ignoring possible socio-economic information. Abel was made less profitable than Jabel. The first packet is referred to as the *conventional treatment*.

2. The second packet includes the same statements, with, in addition, footnotes pertaining to the abatement costs of pollution by the two firms. Abel was made again less profitable than Jabel. However, the difference in profitability was due to different pollution control policy. Abel was shown with a higher amount for pollution abatement resulting in the difference in profitability. The second packet is referred to as the *footnote treatment*.

3. The third packet includes again the same statements, with, in addition, information on the pollution abatement costs disclosed in both the profit-and-loss statement and the footnotes. This treatment is referred to as the *total treatment*.

Each packet includes the financial statements and a questionnaire. Exhibits 7.1 to 7.3 show, respectively, a copy of the financial statements of Abel and Jabel under the conventional, footnote, and total treatments.

In conducting the experiment for each of the subject groups, it was specifically requested that the three packets be distributed randomly so that each member of a group received one and only one of the packets. The criterion variable was obtained by asking the participants to allocate

## Exhibit 7.1
## Financial Statements, Conventional Treatment

(a) Jabel Chemical Inc.

CONSOLIDATED BALANCE SHEET as of December 31

| | 1970 | 1969 |
|---|---|---|
| ASSETS | | |
| Current Assets | | |
| Cash | $ 579,000 | 658,000 |
| Certificates of deposit | 392,000 | – |
| Marketable securities, at cost, which approximates market | 899,000 | – |
| Receivables | 3,500,000 | 2,950,000 |
| Inventories, at lower of average cost of market | 3,400,000 | 3,300,000 |
| Prepayments | 246,000 | 150,000 |
| Total current assets | 9,016,000 | 7,058,000 |
| Plant and Equipment, at cost | | |
| Land | 350,000 | 194,000 |
| Buildings and equipment | 14,550,000 | 13,482,000 |
| Returnable containers | 620,000 | 455,000 |
| | 15,520,000 | 14,131,000 |
| Less – Accumulated depreciation | 7,520,000 | 6,580,000 |
| Patents, Trademarks and Goodwill, in process of amortization | 186,000 | 196,000 |
| | 17,202,000 | 14,805,000 |
| LIABILITIES | | |
| Current Liabilities | | |
| Accounts payable | 2,074,000 | 1,495,000 |
| Dividends payable | 130,000 | 120,000 |
| Accrued liabilities | 598,000 | 480,000 |
| Accrued Federal income taxes | 520,000 | 190,000 |
| Customers' deposits on returnable containers | 450,000 | 380,000 |
| Total current liabilities | 3,772,000 | 2,665,000 |
| Deferred Income Taxes | 1,005,000 | 821,000 |
| Deferred Investment Credit, being amortized over life of related equipment | 320,000 | 331,000 |
| | 5,097,000 | 3,817,000 |

*Source*: Ahmed Belkaoui, "The Impact of Socio-Economic Accounting Statements on the Investment Decision: An Empirical Study," *Accounting, Organizations and Society* 5, no. 3 (1980), pp. 267–270. Reprinted with permission from *Accounting, Organizations and Society*.

## Exhibit 7.1 (continued)

| | | |
|---|---:|---:|
| Stockholders' Investment | | |
| 5% non-cumulative preferred stock, | | |
| $100 par value — authorized | | |
| 6500 shares; outstanding 5491 | | |
| shares in 1970 and 5642 in 1969 | 549,000 | 564,000 |
| Common stock, $2 par value, authorized | | |
| 1,000,000 shares; outstanding 647,620 | | |
| in 1970 and 1969 | 1,295,000 | 1,295,000 |
| Paid in surplus | 42,000 | 39,000 |
| Retained Earnings | 10,219,000 | 9,090,000 |
| Total stockholders' investment | 12,105,000 | 10,988,000 |
| | 17,202,000 | 14,805,000 |

| | 1970 | 1969 |
|---|---:|---:|
| Net Sales | 29,100,000 | 23,400,000 |
| Costs and Expenses | | |
| Cost of goods sold | 19,900,000 | 16,300,000 |
| Selling, general and administrative | 3,600,000 | 2,300,000 |
| Research, development and technical service | 780,000 | 700,000 |
| Depreciation | 955,000 | 860,000 |
| Provision for income taxes | 1,858,000 | 1,294,000 |
| | 27,093,000 | 21,454,000 |
| Net Income | 2,007,000 | 1,946,000 |
| Dividends on Preferred Stock | | |
| ($5 per share) | 28,000 | 28,000 |
| Net Income on Common Stock | 1,979,000 | 1,918,000 |
| Retained Earnings, Beginning of Year | 9,620,000 | 8,100,000 |
| Dividends on Common Stock | | |
| (68–1/2¢ per share and 61–1/2¢ per share) | 444,000 | 398,000 |
| Retained Earnings, End of Year | 11,155,000 | 9,620,000 |
| Net Income per Common Share | 3.09 | 2.9 |

### Four Year Summary

| | 1970 | 1969 | 1968 | 1967 |
|---|---:|---:|---:|---:|
| Net Sales | 29,100,000 | 23,400,000 | 23,404,000 | 18,700,000 |
| Net Income | 2,007,000 | 1,946,000 | 1,500,000 | 1,009,000 |
| Total Assets | 17,202,000 | 14,805,000 | 13,486,000 | 11,659,000 |
| Per Share of | | | | |
| Common Stock | | | | |
| Net Income | 3.09 | 2.9 | 2.28 | 1.51 |
| Dividends declared | 0.68–1/2 | 0.61–1/2 | 0.48 | 0.38 |
| Price Range | | | | |
| Com. (OTC Bid) | 42–23 | 29–20 | 24–16 | 20–14 |

**Exhibit 7.1** (continued)

(b) Abel Chemical Inc.

CONSOLIDATED BALANCE SHEET, as of December 31

| | 1970 | 1969 |
|---|---|---|
| ASSETS | | |
| Current Assets | | |
| Cash | 579,000 | 658,000 |
| Certificates of deposit | 392,000 | – |
| Marketable securities, at cost, | | |
| which approximates market | 899,000 | – |
| Receivables | 3,393,000 | 2,938,000 |
| Inventories, at lower of average | | |
| cost of market | 3,327,000 | 3,411,000 |
| Prepayments | 246,000 | 149,000 |
| Total current assets | 8,836,000 | 7,156,000 |
| | | |
| Plant and Equipment at cost | | |
| Land | 334,000 | 194,000 |
| Buildings and equipment | 14,151,000 | 13,482,000 |
| Returnable containers | 587,000 | 455,000 |
| | 15,072,000 | 14,131,000 |
| Less – Accumulated depreciation | 7,424,000 | 6,580,000 |
| | 7,648,000 | 7,551,000 |
| Patents, Trademarks and Goodwill, | | |
| in process of amortization | 172,000 | 196,000 |
| | 16,656,000 | 14,903,000 |
| LIABILITIES | | |
| Current Liabilities | | |
| Accounts payable | 1,566,000 | 1,609,000 |
| Dividends payable | 130,000 | 114,000 |
| Accrued liabilities | 598,000 | 480,000 |
| Accrued federal income taxes | 508,000 | 185,000 |
| Customers' deposits on returnable containers | 424,000 | 375,000 |
| Total current liabilities | 3,226,000 | 2,763,000 |
| Deferred Income Taxes | 1,005,000 | 821,000 |
| Deferred Investment Credit, being amortized | | |
| over life of related equipment | 320,000 | 331,000 |
| | 4,551,000 | 3,915,000 |

Exhibit 7.1 (continued)

| Stockholders' Investment | | |
|---|---|---|
| 5% non-cumulative preferred stock, $100 par value – authorized 6500 shares; outstanding 5491 in 1970 and 5642 in 1969 | 549,000 | 564,000 |
| Common stock, $2 par value – authorized 1,000,000 shares; outstanding 647,620 in 1970 and 1969 | 1,295,000 | 1,295,000 |
| Paid-in surplus | 42,000 | 39,000 |
| Retained earnings | 10,219,000 | 9,090,000 |
| .Total stockholders' investment | 12,105,000 | 10,988,000 |
| | 16,656,000 | 14,903,000 |

| | 1970 | 1969 |
|---|---|---|
| Net Sales | 28,169,000 | 22,969,000 |
| Costs and Expenses | | |
| Cost of goods sold | 18,921,000 | 16,389,000 |
| Selling, general and administrative | 3,000,000 | 1,300,000 |
| Research, development and technical service | 1,834,000 | 1,730,000 |
| Depreciation | 955,000 | 856,000 |
| Provision for income taxes | 1,858,000 | 1,294,000 |
| | 26,568,000 | 21,569,000 |
| Net Income | 1,601,000 | 1,400,000 |
| Dividends on Preferred Stock ($5 per share) | 28,000 | 28,000 |
| Net Income on Common Stock | 1,573,000 | 1,372,000 |
| Retained Earnings, Beginning of Year | 9,090,000 | 8,116,000 |
| Dividends on Common Stock (68-1/2 per share and 61-1/2¢ per share) | 444,000 | 398,000 |
| Retained Earnings, End of Year | 10,219,000 | 9,090,000 |
| Net Income Per Common Share | 2.43 | 2.12 |

Four Year Summary

| | | | | |
|---|---|---|---|---|
| Net Sales | 28,169,000 | 22,969,000 | 22,402,000 | 18,649,000 |
| Net Income | 1,601,000 | 1,400,000 | 1,499,000 | 1,007,000 |
| Total Assets | 16,656,000 | 14,903,000 | 13,286,000 | 11,659,000 |
| Per Share of Common Stock: | | | | |
| Net Income | 2.43 | 2.12 | 2.27 | 1.51 |
| Dividends Declared | 0.68-1/2 | 0.61-1/2 | 0.48 | 0.38 |
| Price Range: | | | | |
| Com. (OTC bid) | 42–23 | 29–20 | 24–16 | 20–14 |
| | 1970 | 1969 | 1968 | 1967 |

**Exhibit 7.2**
**Financial Statements, Footnote Treatment**

(a) Jabel Chemical Inc.

| CONSOLIDATED BALANCE SHEET, AS OF DECEMBER 31 | | |
|---|---|---|
| ASSETS | 1970 | 1969 |
| Current Assets | | |
| Cash | $ 579,000 | 658,000 |
| Certificates of deposit | 392,000 | – |
| Marketable securities at cost, | | |
| which approximates market | 899,000 | – |
| Receivables | 3,500,000 | 2,950,000 |
| Inventories, at lower of average | | |
| cost or market | 3,400,000 | 3,300,000 |
| Prepayments | 246,000 | 150,000 |
| Total current assets | 9,016,000 | 7,058,000 |
| Plant and Equipment, at cost (Note 1) | | |
| Land | 350,000 | 194,000 |
| Buildings and equipment | 14,550,000 | 13,482,000 |
| Returnable containers | 620,000 | 455,000 |
| | 15,520,000 | 14,131,000 |
| Less – Accumulated depreciation | 7,520,000 | 6,580,000 |
| | 8,000,000 | 7,551,000 |
| LIABILITIES | | |
| Current Liabilities | | |
| Accounts payable | 2,074,000 | 1,495,000 |
| Dividends payable | 130,000 | 120,000 |
| Accrued liabilities | 598,000 | 480,000 |
| Accrued federal income taxes | 520,000 | 190,000 |
| Customers' deposits on returnable | | |
| containers | 450,000 | 380,000 |
| Total current liabilities | 3,772,000 | 2,665,000 |
| Deferred Income Taxes | 1,005,000 | 821,000 |
| Deferred Investment Credit, being | | |
| amortized over life of related | | |
| equipment | 320,000 | 331,000 |
| | 5,097,000 | 3,817,000 |
| Stockholders' Investment | | |
| 5% non-cumulative preferred stock, | | |
| $100 par value – authorized 6500 | | |
| shares; outstanding 5491 shares in | | |
| 1970 and 5642 in 1969 | 594,000 | 564,000 |
| Common stock, $2 par value – | | |
| authorized 1,000,000 shares, | | |
| outstanding 647,620 in 1970 and | | |
| 1969 | 1,295,000 | 1,295,000 |
| Paid in surplus | 42,000 | 39,000 |
| Retained Earnings | 10,219,000 | 9,090,000 |
| Stockholders' investment | 12,105,000 | 10,988,000 |
| | 17,202,000 | 14,805,000 |

*Source*: Ahmed Belkaoui, "The Impact of Socio-Economic Accounting Statements on the Investment Decision: An Empirical Study," *Accounting, Organizations and Society* 5, no. 3 (1980), pp. 271–273. Reprinted with permission from *Accounting, Organizations and Society*.

Exhibit 7.2 (continued)

| | | |
|---|---|---|
| Net Sales | 29,100,000 | 23,400,000 |
| Costs and Expenses | | |
| Cost of goods sold | 19,900,000 | 16,300,000 |
| Selling, general and administrative | 3,600,000 | 2,300,000 |
| Research, development and | | |
| technical service (Note 2) | 780,000 | 700,000 |
| Depreciation | 955,000 | 860,000 |
| Provision for income taxes | 1,858,000 | 1,294,000 |
| | 27,093,000 | 21,454,000 |
| Net Income | 2,007,000 | 1,946,000 |
| Dividends on Preferred Stock | | |
| ($5 per share) | 28,000 | 28,000 |
| Net Income on Common Stock | 1,979,000 | 1,918,000 |
| Retained Earnings, Beginning of Year | 9,620,000 | 8,100,000 |
| Dividends on Common Stock | | |
| (68-1/2¢ per share and | | |
| 61-1/2¢ per share) | 444,000 | 398,000 |
| Retained Earnings, End of Year | 11,155,000 | 9,620,000 |
| Net Income per Common Share | 3.09 | 2.9 |

The accompanying notes are an integral part of this consolidated statement.

Note 1: Plant and equipment includes $500,000 a year gross capital expenditures for equipment necessary to accommodate less pollutant raw materials and to reduce the emission of contaminants resulting from chemical production.

Note 2: This includes $700,000 a year as utility expenditures for air pollution control as follows:
a) operating costs related to the characteristics of high quality raw materials and to the use of control equipment $350,000 a year
b) R and D expenditures to improve the air pollution control program $350,000 a year.

### Four Year Summary

| | 1970 | 1969 | 1968 | 1969 |
|---|---|---|---|---|
| Net Sales | 29,100,000 | 23,400,000 | 23,404,000 | 18,700,000 |
| Net Income | 2,007,000 | 1,946,000 | 1,500,000 | 1,009,000 |
| Total Assets | 17,202,000 | 14,805,000 | 13,486,000 | 11,659,000 |
| Per share of common stock: | | | | |
| Net income | 3.09 | 2.9 | 2.28 | 1.51 |
| Dividends declared | 0.68-1/2 | 0.61-1/2 | 0.48 | 0.38 |
| Price range Com. (OTC bid) | 42-23 | 29-20 | 24-16 | 20-14 |
| Per share of common stock before pollution expenditures | | | | |
| Net Income | 4.1 | 3.0 | | |

**Exhibit 7.2 (continued)**

(b) Abel Chemical Inc.

CONSOLIDATED BALANCE SHEET, AS OF DECEMBER 31

| ASSETS | 1970 | 1969 |
|---|---|---|
| Current Assets | | |
| Cash | 579,000 | 658,000 |
| Certificates of deposit | 392,000 | – |
| Marketable securities, at cost, | | |
| which approximates market | 899,000 | – |
| Receivables | 3,393,000 | 2,938,000 |
| Inventories, at lower of average cost | | |
| or market | 3,327,000 | 3,411,000 |
| Prepayments | 246,000 | 149,000 |
| Total current assets | 8,836,000 | 7,156,000 |
| Plant and Equipment, at cost (Note 1) | | |
| Land | 334,000 | 194,000 |
| Buildings and equipment | 14,151,000 | 13,482,000 |
| Returnable containers | 587,000 | 455,000 |
| | 15,072,000 | 14,131,000 |
| Less – Accumulated depreciation | 7,424,000 | 6,580,000 |
| | 7,648,000 | 7,551,000 |
| Patents, Trademarks and Goodwill, | | |
| in process of amortization | 172,000 | 196,000 |
| | 16,656,000 | 14,903,000 |
| LIABILITIES | | |
| Current Liabilities | | |
| Accounts payable | 1,566,000 | 1,609,000 |
| Dividends payable | 130,000 | 114,000 |
| Accrued liabilities | 598,000 | 480,000 |
| Accrued federal income taxes | 508,000 | 185,000 |
| Customers' deposits on returnable | | |
| containers | 424,000 | 375,000 |
| Total current liabilities | 3,226,000 | 2,763,000 |
| Deferred Income Taxes | 1,005,000 | 821,000 |
| Deferred Investment Credit, being | | |
| amortized over life of related | | |
| equipment | 320,000 | 331,000 |
| | 4,551,000 | 3,915,000 |
| Stockholders' Investment | | |
| 5% non-cumulative preferred stock, | | |
| $100 par value – authorized 6500 | | |
| shares; outstanding 5491 in 1970 | | |
| and 5642 in 1969 | 549,000 | 564,000 |
| Common stock, $2 par value – | | |
| authorized 1,000,000 shares; | | |
| outstanding 647,620 in 1970 and | | |
| 1969 | 1,295,000 | 1,295,000 |
| Paid-in surplus | 42,000 | 39,000 |
| Retained earnings | 10,219,000 | 9,090,000 |
| Total stockholders' investment | 12,105,000 | 10,988,000 |
| | 16,656,000 | 14,903,000 |

Exhibit 7.2 (continued)

| | | |
|---|---:|---:|
| Net Sales | 28,169,000 | 22,969,000 |
| Costs and Expenses | | |
| Cost of goods sold | 18,921,000 | 16,389,000 |
| Selling, general and administrative | 3,000,000 | 1,300,000 |
| Research, development and | | |
| technical service (Note 2) | 1,834,000 | 1,730,000 |
| Depreciation | 955,000 | 856,000 |
| Provision for income taxes | 1,858,000 | 1,294,000 |
| | 26,568,000 | 21,569,000 |
| Net Income | 1,601,000 | 1,400,000 |
| Dividends on Preferred Stock | | |
| ($5 per share) | 28,000 | 28,000 |
| Net Income on Common Stock | 1,573,000 | 1,372,000 |
| Retained Earnings, Beginning of Year | 9,090,000 | 8,116,000 |
| Dividends on Common Stock | 444,000 | 398,000 |
| (68–1/2¢ per share and | | |
| 61–1/2¢ per share) | | |
| Retained Earnings, End of Year | 10,219,000 | 9,090,000 |
| Net Income per Common Share | 2.43 | 2.12 |

The accompanying notes are an integral part of this consolidated statement.

Note 1: Plant and equipment includes $650,000 a year capital expenditures for equipment necessary to accommodate less pollutant inputs and to reduce the emission of contaminants resulting from chemical production.

Note 2: This includes $1,730,000 a year as utility expenditures for air pollution control as follows:
a) operating costs related to the characteristics of high quality raw materials and to the use of control equipment $1,020,000 a year.
b) R and D expenditures to improve the air pollution control program $710,000 a year.

## Four Year Summary

| | | | | |
|---|---:|---:|---:|---:|
| Net Sales | 28,169,000 | 22,969,000 | 22,402,000 | 18,649,000 |
| Net Income | 1,601,000 | 1,400,000 | 1,499,000 | 1,007,000 |
| Total Assets | 16,656,000 | 14,903,000 | 13,286,000 | 11,659,000 |
| Per Share of | | | | |
| Common Stock: | | | | |
| Net Income | 2.43 | 2.12 | 2.27 | 1.51 |
| Dividends Declared | 0.68–1/2 | 0.61–1/2 | 0.48 | 0.38 |
| Price Range: | | | | |
| Com. (OTC bid) | 42–23 | 29–20 | 24–16 | 20–14 |
| Per share of | | | | |
| Common stock | | | | |
| Before pollution | | | | |
| Expenditures | | | | |
| Net income | 5.1 | 4.8 | — | — |

a certain amount of money between the two companies, Abel and Jabel, under two investment strategies. The main instructions read as follows:

> We are providing you with information packets concerning JABEL CHEMICAL INC. and ABEL CHEMICAL INC. These are two fictional chemical companies. On the basis of the information available to you, you have been asked to help Mr. John Smith make a portfolio decision between these two companies.
>
> Mr. Smith, who has been investing in non-chemical companies, has $30,000 in cash which he would like to invest in common stock of chemical companies. Following analysis of the information provided on the two investment alternatives, what proportion of each common stock would you advise Mr. Smith to buy if:
> Case A—Mr. Smith wishes to invest for income reasons?
> Case B—Mr. Smith wishes to invest for capital growth?

The main instructions were followed by the financial statements of Abel and Jabel and the following question:

> Now that you had a chance to evaluate both ABEL CHEMICAL INC. and JABEL CHEMICAL INC. what proportion of the $30,000 would you advise Mr. Smith to invest in each firm respectively if:
> a) Mr. Smith wishes to invest for income reasons?
> b) Mr. Smith wishes to invest for capital growth?

The participants were also explained the differences in the two investment strategies to insure uniformity of interpretation.

### The Perceptual and Background Variables

To investigate the fourth hypothesis pertaining to the possible association between the investment decisions and perceptual and background variables, the following variables are selected:

1. the age of the subject;
2. the number of college-level courses in accounting and finance;
3. the extent to which portfolio selection is an important part of his job;

**Exhibit 7.3**
**Financial Statements, Total Treatment**

(a) Jabel Chemical Inc.

CONSOLIDATED BALANCE SHEET, as of December 31

| ASSETS | 1970 | 1969 |
|---|---|---|
| Current Assets | | |
| Cash | 579,000 | 658,000 |
| Certificates of deposit | 392,000 | – |
| Marketable securities, at cost, | | |
| which approximates market | 899,000 | – |
| Receivables | 3,500,000 | 2,950,000 |
| Inventories at lower of average | | |
| cost or market | 3,400,000 | 3,300,000 |
| Prepayments | 246,000 | 150,000 |
| Total current assets | 9,016,000 | 7,058,000 |
| Plant and Equipment (Note 1) | | |
| Land | 350,000 | 194,000 |
| Buildings and equipment | 14,550,000 | 13,482,000 |
| Returnable containers | 620,000 | 455,000 |
| | 15,520,000 | 14,131,000 |
| Less – Accumulated depreciation | 7,520,000 | 6,580,000 |
| | 8,000,000 | 7,551,000 |
| Patents, Trademarks and Goodwill, | | |
| in process of amortization | 186,000 | 196,000 |
| | 17,202,000 | 14,805,000 |
| LIABILITIES | | |
| Current Liabilities | | |
| Accounts payable | 2,074,000 | 1,495,000 |
| Dividends payable | 130,000 | 120,000 |
| Accrued liabilities | 598,000 | 480,000 |
| Accrued federal income taxes | 520,000 | 190,000 |
| Customers' deposits on returnable | | |
| containers | 450,000 | 380,000 |
| Total current liabilities | 3,772,000 | 2,665,000 |
| Deferred Income Taxes | 1,005,000 | 821,000 |
| Deferred Investment Credit, being | | |
| amortized over life of related | | |
| equipment | 320,000 | 331,000 |
| Stockholders' Investment | 5,097,000 | 3,817,000 |
| 5% non-cumulative preferred stock, | | |
| $100 par value – authorized 6500 | | |
| shares; outstanding 5491 shares in | | |
| 1970 and 5642 in 1969 | 594,000 | 564,000 |
| Common stock, $2 par value – | | |
| authorized 1,000,000 shares, | | |
| outstanding 647,620 in 1970 and | | |
| 1969 | 1,295,000 | 1,295,000 |
| Paid in surplus | 42,000 | 39,000 |
| Retained earnings | 10,219,000 | 9,090,000 |
| Total stockholders' investment | 12,105,000 | 10,988,000 |
| | 17,202,000 | 14,805,000 |

*Source*: Ahmed Belkaoui, ''The Impact of Socio-Economic Accounting Statements on the Investment Decision: An Empirical Study,'' *Accounting, Organizations and Society* 5, no. 3 (1980),
pp. 273–275. Reprinted with permission from *Accounting, Organizations and Society*.

**Exhibit 7.3** (continued)

|  | 1970 | 1969 |
|---|---|---|
| Net Sales | 29,100,000 | 23,400,000 |
| Costs and Expenses |  |  |
|    Costs of goods sold | 19,900,000 | 16,300,000 |
|    Selling, general and administrative | 3,680,000 | 2,300,000 |
|    Abatement costs of pollution |  |  |
|      (Note 2) | 700,000 | 700,000 |
|    Depreciation | 955,000 | 860,000 |
|    Provision for income taxes | 1,858,000 | 1,294,000 |
|  | 27,093,000 | 21,454,000 |
| Net Income | 2,007,000 | 1,946,000 |
| Dividends on Preferred Stock |  |  |
|    ($5 per share) | 28,000 | 28,000 |
| Net Income on Common Stock | 1,979,000 | 1,918,000 |
| Retained Earnings, Beginning of Year | 9,620,000 | 8,100,000 |
| Dividends on Commo 1 Stock |  |  |
|    (68-1/2¢ per share and |  |  |
|    61-1/2¢ per share) | 444,000 | 398,000 |
| Retained Earnings, End of Year | 11,155,000 | 9,620,000 |
| Net Income per Common Share | 3.09 | 2.9 |

The accompanying notes are an integral part of this consolidated statement.

Note 1: Plant and equipment includes $500,000 a year gross capital expenditures for equipment necessary to accommodate less pollutant raw materials and to reduce the emission of contaminants resulting from chemical production.

Note 2: This includes $700,000 a year as utility expenditures for air pollution controls as follows:

a) operating costs related to the characteristics of high quality raw materials and to the use of control equipment – $350,000 a year.

b) R and D expenditures to improve the air pollution control program $350,000 a year.

### Four Year Summary

|  | 1970 | 1969 | 1968 | 1967 |
|---|---|---|---|---|
| Net Sales | 29,100,000 | 23,400,000 | 23,404,000 | 18,700,000 |
| Net Income | 2,007,000 | 1,946,000 | 1,500,000 | 1,009,000 |
| Total Assets | 17,202,000 | 14,805,000 | 13,486,000 | 11,659,000 |
| Per Share of |  |  |  |  |
|   Common Stocks |  |  |  |  |
|   Net Income | 3.09 | 2.9 | 2.28 | 1.51 |
| Dividends Declared | 0.68-1/2 | 0.61-1/2 | 0.48 | 0.38 |
| Price Range |  |  |  |  |
|   Com (OTC bid) | 42-23 | 29-20 | 24-16 | 20-14 |
| Per Share of |  |  |  |  |
|   Common Stock |  |  |  |  |
|   Before Pollution |  |  |  |  |
|   Expenditures | 4.1 | 3.0 | – | – |

**Exhibit 7.3 (continued)**

(b) Abel Chemical Inc.

CONSOLIDATED BALANCE SHEET, as of December 31

| ASSETS | 1970 | 1969 |
|---|---|---|
| Current Assets | | |
| Cash | 579,000 | 658,000 |
| Certificates of deposit | 392,000 | – |
| Marketable securities, at cost, which approximates market | 899,000 | – |
| Receivables | 3,393,000 | 2,938,000 |
| Inventories, at lower of average cost or market | 3,327,000 | 3,411,000 |
| Prepayments | 246,000 | 149,000 |
| Total current assets | 8,836,000 | 7,156,000 |
| Plant and equipment at cost (Note 1) | | |
| Land | 334,000 | 194,000 |
| Buildings and equipment | 14,151,000 | 13,482,000 |
| Returnable containers | 587,000 | 455,000 |
| | 15,072,000 | 14,131,000 |
| Less – Accumulated depreciation | 7,424,000 | 6,580,000 |
| | 7,648,000 | 7,551,000 |
| Patents, Trademarks and Goodwill, in process of amortization | 172,000 | 196,000 |
| LIABILITIES | | |
| Current Liabilities | | |
| Accounts payable | 1,566,000 | 1,609,000 |
| Dividends payable | 130,000 | 114,000 |
| Accrued liabilities | 598,000 | 480,000 |
| Accrued federal income taxes | 508,000 | 185,000 |
| Customers' deposits on returnable containers | 424,000 | 375,000 |
| Total current liabilities | 3,226,000 | 2,763,000 |
| Deferred Income Taxes | 1,005,000 | 821,000 |
| Deferred Investment Credit, being amortized over life of related equipment | 320,000 | 331,000 |
| | 4,551,000 | 3,915,000 |
| Stockholders' Investment | | |
| 5% non-cumulative preferred stock, $100 par value – authorized 6500 shares: outstanding 5491 in 1971 and 5642 in 1969 | 549,000 | 564,000 |
| Common Stock, $2 par value – authorized 1,000,000 shares; outstanding 647,620 in 1970 and 1969 | 1,295,000 | 1,295,000 |
| Paid in surplus | 42,000 | 39,000 |
| Retained earnings | 10,219,000 | 9,090,000 |
| Total stockholders' investment | 12,105,000 | 10,988,000 |
| | 16,656,000 | 14,903,000 |

**Exhibit 7.3 (continued)**

|  | 1970 | 1969 |
|---|---|---|
| Net Sales | 28,169,000 | 22,969,000 |
| Costs and Expenses |  |  |
| Cost of goods sold | 18,921,000 | 16,389,000 |
| Selling, general and administrative | 2,104,000 | 1,300,000 |
| Abatement costs of pollution |  |  |
| (Note 2) | 1,730,000 | 1,730,000 |
| Depreciation | 955,000 | 856,000 |
| Provision for income taxes | 1,858,000 | 1,294,000 |
|  | 26,568,000 | 21,569,000 |
| Net Income | 1,601,000 | 1,400,000 |
| Dividends on Preferred Stock |  |  |
| ($5 per share) | 28,000 | 28,000 |
| Net Income on Common Stock | 1,573,000 | 1,372,000 |
| Retained Earnings, Beginning of Year | 9,090,000 | 8,116,000 |
| Dividends on Common Stock |  |  |
| (68-1/2¢ per share and |  |  |
| 61-1/2¢ per share) | 444,000 | 398,000 |
| Retained Earnings, End of Year | 10,219,000 | 9,090,000 |
| Net Income per Common Share | 2.43 | 2.12 |

The accompanying notes are an integral part of this consolidated statement.

Note 1: Plant and equipment includes $650,000 a year capital expenditures for equipment necessary to accommodate less pollutant inputs to reduce the emission of contaminants resulting from chemical production.

Note 2: This includes $1,730,000 a year as utility expenditures for air pollution control as follows:

a) operating costs related to the characteristics of high quality raw materials and to the use of control equipment – $1,020,000 a year.

b) R and D expenditures to the art of air pollution control program, $710,000 a year.

**Four Year Summary**

|  | 1970 | 1969 | 1968 | 1967 |
|---|---|---|---|---|
| Net Sales | 28,169,000 | 22,969,000 | 22,402,000 | 18,649,000 |
| Net Income | 1,601,000 | 1,400,000 | 1,499,000 | 1,007,000 |
| Total Assets | 16,656,000 | 14,903,000 | 13,286,000 | 11,659,000 |
| Per Share of |  |  |  |  |
| Common Stock: |  |  |  |  |
| Net Income | 2.43 | 2.12 | 2.27 | 1.51 |
| Dividends Declared | 0.68-1/2 | 0.61-1/2 | 0.48 | 0.38 |
| Price Range: |  |  |  |  |
| Com. (OTC bid) | 42-23 | 29-20 | 24-16 | 20-14 |
| Per Share of |  |  |  |  |
| Common Stock |  |  |  |  |
| Before Pollution |  |  |  |  |
| Expenditures |  |  |  |  |
| Net Income | 5.1 | 4.8 | – | – |

4. the degree of acceptance of the disclosure of the abatement costs of pollution to improve the investment decisions;

5. the number of years in which the participant was engaged in evaluating financial statements;

6. the perception of the importance of the issue of "ecological crisis";

7. the tradeoff between pollution control and profitability.

These variables were included in a questionnaire to be answered after completion of the main experimental portfolio decision task. Because the subjects might be sensitized to the experimental variables if they glanced through the complete questionnaire before responding to the individual questions, especially for subjects receiving statements with abatement costs in either the footnote or the total treatments, they were warned and reminded explicitly in the questionnaire as a basic condition to the validity of the experiment to respond to the experimental task before continuing with the questionnaire. In addition, it was insured that a reinforcement of this warning was made by the administrators of the experiment for the three groups.

### The Experimental Design

A split-plot design is used in this study. It includes three factors: two between variables each one at three levels, and one within variables at two levels. They were: (1) the membership to occupational group as the first between variable (Factor $A$) with level $a_1$ for accountants, level $a_2$ for bankers, and level $a_3$ for students, (2) the accounting treatment as the second between variable (Factor $B$) with $b_1$ as the conventional treatment, $b_2$ as the footnote treatment, and $b_3$ as the total treatment, and (3) the investment policy as the within variable (Factor $C$) with $C_1$ as the investment for dividend income and $C_2$ as the investment for capital gains. This is a design where there are repeated measures on only one of the three factors, namely the investment strategy, resulting in eighteen cells. The design is shown in Exhibit 7.4.

Each of the groups was observed under both levels of $C$, i.e., investment policies. *But each group was assigned to only one combination of Factors* $A$ *and* B. The notation $S_{ij}$ denotes the groups of participants assigned to the treatment combination $ab_{ij}$ with the participant effect nested under $A$ and $B$.

**Exhibit 7.4**
**3 × 3 × 2 × N Split-Plot Design**

| Factor $A$ – Occupational Group | Factor $B$ – Accounting Treatments | Factor $C$ – Investment Strategy | |
|---|---|---|---|
| | | $C_1$ (Income) | $C_2$ (Capital Gains) |
| $a_1$ – accountants | $b_1$ – conventional | $S_{11}$ | $S_{11}$ |
| | $b_2$ – footnote | $S_{12}$ | $S_{12}$ |
| | $b_3$ – total | $S_{13}$ | $S_{13}$ |
| $a_2$ – bankers | $b_1$ – conventional | $S_{14}$ | $S_{14}$ |
| | $b_2$ – footnote | $S_{22}$ | $S_{22}$ |
| | $b_3$ – total | $S_{23}$ | $S_{23}$ |
| $a_3$ – students | $b_1$ – conventional | $S_{31}$ | $S_{31}$ |
| | $b_2$ – footnote | $S_{32}$ | $S_{32}$ |
| | $b_3$ – total | $S_{33}$ | $S_{33}$ |

*Source*: Ahmed Belkaoui, "The Impact of Socio-Economic Accounting Statements on the Investment Decision: An Empirical Study," *Accounting, Organizations and Society* 5, no. 3 (1980), p. 276. Reprinted with permission from *Accounting, Organizations and Society*.

**Exhibit 7.5**
**Analysis of Variance**

| | Source | df | SS | MS | F | Significant level |
|---|---|---|---|---|---|---|
| | | | Analysis of variance (2 Between, 1 Within) | | | |
| Subjects | | 224 | 199.730 | | | |
| A. | Occupational group | 2 | 5.303 | 2.651 | 3.200 | * |
| B. | Accounting treatments | 2 | 6.196 | 3.098 | 3.739 | * |
| AB. | | 4 | 9.245 | 9.311 | 2.789 | * |
| E(AB). | | 216 | 178.986 | 0.879 | | |
| C. | Investment strategy | 1 | 17.036 | 17.036 | 33.468 | * |
| AC. | | 2 | 7.539 | 3.769 | 7.405 | * |
| BC. | | 2 | 5.492 | 2.746 | 5.395 | * |
| ABC. | | 4 | 5.318 | 1.379 | 2.612 | * |
| E(ABC). | | 216 | 109.947 | 0.509 | | |
| W. | | 225 | 145.311 | | | |
| Total | | 450 | 1056.326 | | | |

*Significant at $a = 0.05$.

*Source*: Ahmed Belkaoui, "The Impact of Socio-Economic Accounting Statements on the Investment Decision: An Empirical Study," *Accounting, Organizations and Society* 5, no. 3 (1980), p. 277. Reprinted with permission from *Accounting, Organizations and Society*.

The structure model on which the analysis is based has the following form.

$$X_{ijkm} = + \alpha_i + \beta_j + \alpha\beta_{ij} + \pi_n(ij) + \gamma_k + \alpha\gamma_{ik}$$
$$+ \beta\gamma_{jk} + \alpha\beta\gamma_{ijk} + \gamma\pi_{km(ij)} + O(ijkm)$$

where:

$X_{ijkm}$ = percentage invested in Jabel Chemical Inc. after an arcsine transformation

$\alpha_i$ = effect of treatment $A$, which is a constant for all subjects within treatment population $i$

$\beta_j$ = effect of treatment $B$, which is a constant for all subjects within treatment population $j$

$\alpha\beta_{ij}$ = effect that represents nonadditivity of effects and $B_j$

$\pi_n(ij)$ = effect of subject $n$, which is nested under level $ab_{ij}$

$\gamma_k$ = effect of treatment $C$, which is a constant for all subjects within treatment population $k$

$\alpha\gamma_{ik}$ = effect that represents nonadditivity of effects $\alpha_i$ and $\gamma_k$

$\beta\gamma_{jk}$ = effect that represents nonadditivity of effects $\alpha_i$, $\beta_j$, and $\gamma_k$

$\gamma\pi_{km(ij)}$ = effect that represents nonadditivity of effects $\gamma_k$ and $\pi_{km(ij)}$

$O$ = experimental error

To meet the assumption implicit in the use of analysis of variance, a change in the scale of measurement of the criterion was deemed appropriate. Because our observations were proportions, they were transformed on the basis of an arcsine transformation.


## RESULTS

### The Impact of the Experimental Factors

Exhibits 7.5 and 7.6. portray, respectively, the results of the analysis of variance and the table of means testing the implicit null hypothesis of "no effect" for the three experimental factors and their interactions. All main effects and interactions effects were significant at a 0.05 level leading to the acceptance of this chapter's first hypothesis, namely:

**Exhibit 7.6**
**Table of Means**

| | | C1 | C2 |
|---|---|---|---|
| | | *A B C* | |
| | | Summary Table | |
| $B_1$ $A_1$ | $B_1$ | 1.561 | 1.499 |
| | $B_2$ | 1.849 | 0.930 |
| | $B_3$ | 1.912 | 0.631 |
| | $B_1$ | 2.210 | 1.959 |
| $A_2$ | $B_2$ | 1.486 | 1.355 |
| | $B_3$ | 1.630 | 1.334 |
| | $B_1$ | 1.496 | 1.465 |
| $A_3$ | $B_2$ | 1.609 | 1.474 |
| | $B_3$ | 1.788 | 1.394 |

*Source*: Ahmed Belkaoui, "The Impact of Socio-Economic Accounting Statements on the Investment Decision: An Empirical Study," *Accounting, Organizations and Society* 5, no. 3 (1980), p. 277. Reprinted with permission from *Accounting, Organizations and Society*.

1. The accounting treatment of pollution control expenditures (conventional, footnote, or total treatment) had a significant impact on the subject's investment decision ($F = 3.200$, $p = 0.05$).

2. The three subject types, belonging to three different occupational groups, did differ significantly in terms of their investment decision ($F = 3.739$, $p = 0.05$).

3. The investment strategy of the subject (investing for dividend income or investing for capital gains) was a significant determinant of the subject's investment decision ($F = 33.468$, $p = 0.05$).

In fact, when interactions are significant, additional insight into the effects of factor treatment can be achieved by analyzing simple main effects. Results of these simple main effects are illustrated in Exhibit 7.7. In what follows, the most salient relationships are discussed:

1. The accounting treatment for pollution control had a significant impact on the subject's investment decision when the bankers were investing for income ($F = 3.487$, $p = 0.05$) and when the

**Exhibit 7.7**
**Summary of Simple Main Effects**

| Effects | df | SS | MS | F | Significance |
|---|---|---|---|---|---|
| $AB$ at $c_1$ | 4 | 9.467 | 2.367 | 3.658 | † |
| $B$ at $a_1 c_1$ | 2 | 1.980 | 0.990 | 1.941 | |
| $B$ at $a_2 c_1$ | 2 | 6.525 | 3.262 | 3.487 | † |
| $B$ at $a_3 c_1$ | 2 | 0.569 | 0.284 | 0.551 | |
| $A$ at $b_1 c_1$ | 2 | 8.677 | 4.339 | 7.299 | † |
| $A$ at $b_2 c_1$ | 2 | 1.672 | 0.836 | 1.692 | |
| $A$ at $b_3 c_1$ | 2 | 0.995 | 0.497 | 0.562 | |
| $AB$ at $c_2$ | 4 | 5.095 | 1.274 | 1.844 | |
| $B$ at $a_1 c_2$ | 2 | 8.793 | 4.396 | 8.837 | † |
| $B$ at $a_2 c_2$ | 2 | 5.523 | 2.761 | 3.202 | † |
| $B$ at $a_3 c_2$ | 2 | 0.144 | 0.072 | 0.098 | |
| $A$ at $b_1 c_2$ | 2 | 5.155 | 2.578 | 3.546 | † |
| $A$ at $b_2 c_2$ | 2 | 4.552 | 2.276 | 3.438 | † |
| $A$ at $b_3 c_2$ | 2 | 9.168 | 4.584 | 6.491 | † |
| $BC$ at $a_1$ | 2 | 9.758 | 4.879 | 10.893 | † |
| $B$ at $a_1 c_1$ | 2 | 1.980 | 0.990 | 1.941 | |
| $B$ at $a_1 c_2$ | 2 | 8.793 | 4.396 | 8.837 | † |
| $C$ at $a_1 b_1$ | 1 | 56.250 | 56.250 | 62.27 | † |
| $C$ at $a_1 b_2$ | 1 | 52.250 | 52.250 | 55.70 | † |
| $C$ at $a_1 b_3$ | 1 | 54.500 | 54.500 | 60.50 | † |
| $BC$ at $a_2$ | 2 | 0.181 | 0.090 | 0.164 | |
| $B$ at $a_2$ | 2 | 13.477 | 6.732 | 5.283 | † |
| $C$ at $a_2$ | 1 | 1.917 | 1.917 | 3.480 | † |
| $BC$ at $a_3$ | 2 | 0.873 | 0.436 | 0.826 | |
| $B$ at $a_3$ | 2 | 0.304 | 0.152 | 0.243 | |
| $C$ at $a_3$ | 1 | 1.308 | 1.308 | 2.477 | |
| $AC$ at $b_1$ | 2 | 0.352 | 0.176 | 0.464 | † |
| $A$ at $b_1$ | 2 | 11.267 | 5.634 | 6.100 | |
| $C$ at $b_1$ | 2 | 0.501 | 0.501 | 1.320 | † |
| $AC$ at $b_2$ | 2 | 5.272 | 2.636 | 5.103 | |
| $A$ at $b_2 c_1$ | 2 | 1.672 | 0.836 | 1.692 | † |
| $A$ at $b_2 c_2$ | 2 | 4.552 | 2.276 | 3.438 | † |
| $C$ at $a_1 b_2$ | 1 | 52.250 | 52.250 | 55.70 | † |
| $C$ at $a_2 b_2$ | 1 | 42.25 | 42.25 | 46.60 | † |
| $C$ at $a_3 b_2$ | 1 | 51.25 | 51.25 | 54.60 | † |
| $AC$ at $b_3$ | 2 | 7.587 | 3.793 | 5.823 | † |
| $A$ at $c_1 b_3$ | 2 | 0.995 | 0.497 | 0.562 | |
| $A$ at $c_2 b_3$ | 2 | 9.168 | 4.584 | 6.491 | † |
| $C$ at $a_1 b_3$ | 1 | 54.500 | 54.500 | 60.50 | † |
| $C$ at $a_2 b_3$ | 1 | 64.100 | 64.100 | 71.100 | † |
| $C$ at $a_3 b_3$ | 1 | 58.100 | 58.100 | 64.050 | † |

*$A$ = Professional group          $b_1$ = Conventional treatment
$B$ = Accounting treatment          $b_2$ = Footnote treatment
$C$ = Investment strategy          $b_3$ = Total treatment
$a_1$ = Bankers          $c_1$ = Investment for income
$a_2$ = Accountants          $c_2$ = Investment for capital gains
$a_3$ = Students

†Significant at = 0.05.

Source: Ahmed Belkaoui, ''The Impact of Socio-Economic Accounting Statements on the Investment Decision: An Empirical Study,'' *Accounting, Organizations and Society* 5, no. 3 (1980), p. 278. Reprinted with permission from *Accounting, Organizations and Society*.

accountants and bankers were investing for capital gains ($F = 8.837$, $p = 0.05$; $F = 3.202$, $p = 0.05$).

2. The three subject types differed in their investment decisions when given the conventional treatment and investing for income ($F = 7.299$, $p = 0.05$) and when given any accounting treatment and investing for capital gains ($F = 3.546$, $p = 0.05$; $F = 3.438$, $p = 0.05$; $F = 6.491$, $p = 0.05$).

3. The subject's investment strategy had a significant impact on his or her investment decision in all cases.

### The Impact of the Background and Perceptual Variables

For better interpretation the fourth hypothesis was divided as follows:

$H_{4a}$:  Under the conventional treatment, the subject's investment decision is not associated with each of the background and perceptual variables.

$H_{4b}$:  Under the footnote and total treatment for pollution control information, the subject's investment decision is not associated with each of the background and perceptual variables.

The problem put by these two hypothesis is to determine the degree of association between two sets of attributes. The first attribute is the investment decision as measured by the choice made by the subject between Jabel and Abel in terms of the higher percentage invested in both firms. In other words, if the subject elected to invest a higher percentage of the funds in a given company that company was considered his investment choice. The second attribute is the level of the background variable or the extent of agreement with a perceptual variable. The degree of association between these two sets of attributes is measured by the contingency coefficient $C$. In what follows the most salient relationships are discussed:

1. With one exception, no significant relationships were found between the investment decision and the different levels of each of the background variables under the conventional accounting treatment. The only exception involves the association between the number of college-level courses in accounting and finance and the conventional accounting treatment ($C = 0.3164$, $p = 0.05$).

2. However, with two exceptions, significant relationships were found between the investment decision and the different levels of each of the background variables under both the footnote and the total treatment. The investment decisions under the footnote treatment and the total treatment were significantly associated with the age of the participant ($C =$ 0.1540, $p = 0.05$; $C = 0.3028$, $p = 0.05$), the degree of acceptance of the disclosure of abatement costs of pollution to improve the investment decisions ($C = 0.3510$, $p = 0.05$; $C = 0.2006$, $p = 0.05$), the number of years engaged in evaluating financial statements ($C = 0.3244$, $p = 0.05$; $C = 0.02305$, $p = 0.05$), the importance of the issue of the ecological crisis ($C = 0.3384$, $p = 0.05$, $C = 0.2561$, $p = 0.05$), the tradeoff between pollution control and profitability ($C = 0.1911$, $p = 0.05$; $C = 0.4910$, $p = 0.001$). The two exceptions involve the absence of association between the number of college-level courses taken in accounting and finance and the degree to which portfolio selection is an important part of the subject's job and the two accounting treatments.

More explicitly, the older the participant, and the higher the number of years evaluating financial statements, the higher the degree of acceptance of the disclosure of pollution abatement expenditures, the greater the awareness of the "ecological crisis," the higher the acceptance of a tradeoff between pollution control and profitability, and the greater the awareness of the impact of the disclosure of pollution expenditures on the reports.

## DISCUSSION

In this experiment, the forms of the disclosure of socio-economic accounting information, namely the abatement costs of pollution, were investigated as accounting techniques that may influence the investment decisions of potential users. The theoretical rationale stemming from the linguistic relativity paradigm in accounting was that, in general, the accounting techniques may tend to facilitate or render more difficult various (nonlinguistic) managerial behaviors on the part of the users, and that in this particular context the investment decision effects from different professional groups using alternative socio-economic accounting information will be different.

The results show that, in general, the various accounting treatments for pollution control information had an effect on the investment decision. Their effect was mostly significant with the bankers under any investment policy. The accountants reacted to the information only when investing for capital gains, while the students did not perceive the importance of the abatement cost information at all. The bankers seemed to be more aware of the importance of accounting information and specific information. The students and the accountants do not yet seem to perceive the full importance of the abatement costs information on the reports. This result may be due to: (a) the fact that the bankers are held responsible for any resource allocation and this shows their tendency to adopt a more socially oriented investment attitude; (b) the difference in the degree of expertise in investment analysis between the bankers on one side and the accountants and the students on the other side.

In fact, membership in a professional group had an effect on the investment decision. In particular, it had an effect when the investors were presented with conventional treatments under any investment policy. When they were presented with any form of disclosure of abatement costs information, the effect was dependent on the investment policy of the investor. The effect was significant only when the participants were investing for capital gains. It appears that the investors from any professional group become more aware of the importance of abatement costs information only when investing for capital gains.

In general, the investment policy of the participant had an effect on the investment decision of all the participants from any of the professional groups represented. However, the investment policy did have a strong effect only when the reports disclosed the abatement costs information in any form. It appears that the investment policies of the investors led to different investment decisions with additional disclosure on the abatement costs of pollution.

Besides the membership in a professional group, the type of accounting treatment for pollution control presented, and the investment policy, the investors' behavior was associated with other demographic and perceptual variables.

Abatement cost information ought to be disclosed completely in the financial statements. Its impact on the investors' behavior has been significant in this experiment, especially for bankers. The additional disclosure of pollution cost information has been used to improve the investment decision, especially for investment for capital gains by most of the participants in this behavioral field experiment.

A field experiment such as the one above is subject to numerous methodological and environmental limitations. The relative accuracy of any of the information in this chapter cannot be discussed without realization of these limitations.

First, the sample taken was limited to the officers of the Syracuse commercial banks, the members of the NAA chapter of Syracuse, and the accounting and finance students of Syracuse University. A more representative sample could be taken from the membership list of the Financial Analysts Federation where participants would include only individuals engaged in stock evaluation work.

Second, the results obtained from this experiment are presented as additional evidence that the addition of pollution control information constitutes an improvement of accounting disclosure.

## SUMMARY AND CONCLUSIONS

This study was motivated by the general interest for the disclosure of socio-economic accounting information. The purpose of the chapter was to report the results of a field experiment testing the effects and interactions of three factors: subject type; accounting treatment of socio-economic accounting information; and investment strategy. The rationale from the linguistic relativity paradigm is that the accounting treatments of socio-economic accounting affect individual investment decisions in a way that depends on the professional group of the user and the investment strategy adopted.

The findings attest to the general relevance of socio-economic accounting information for the bankers under any investment strategy, and for the accountant only under an investment strategy focusing on capital gains. The significant interaction effects between the three examined factors provide a warning about any generalizations to be derived from a similar field experiment. In other words, the informational content of any new information, for instance, socio-economic accounting information, is to be ascertained in terms of its relation to relevant environmental variables. In this chapter, investment for capital gains and membership in the banking profession appeared most associated with the use of the socio-economic accounting information.

## NOTES

1. This chapter has been adapted from Ahmed Belkaoui, "The Impact of Socio-Economic Accounting Statements on the Investment Decision: An Empirical Study," *Accounting, Organizations and Society* 5, no. 3 (1980), pp. 263–283. Reprinted with permission from *Accounting, Organizations and Society*.

2. American Accounting Association, Committee on Accounting for Social Performance, "Report of the Committee on Accounting for Social Performance," *The Accounting Review* LI, Supplement (1976), p. 249.

3. F. A. Beams and Paul E. Fertig, "Pollution Control through Social Cost Conversion," *The Journal of Accounting* (November 1971), pp. 37–42.

4. A. Belkaoui, "The Impact of the Disclosure of the Environment Effects of Organizational Behavior on the Market," *Financial Management* (Winter 1976), pp. 26–31.

5. Joseph H. Bragdon, Jr. and John Marlin, "Is Pollution Profitable?" *Risk Management* (April 1972), pp. 14–32.

6. Barry H. Spicer, "Investors, Corporate Social Performance and Information Disclosure: An Empirical Study," *The Accounting Review* (January 1978), pp. 34–111.

7. J. G. Simon, C. W. Pavers, and J. P. Gunnemann, *The Ethical Investor* (New Haven, Conn.: Yale University Press, 1972).

8. B. Longstreth and H. David Rosenblom, *Social Responsibility and the Institutional Investor* (New York: Praeger, 1973).

9. *Report of the Study Group on Objectives of Financial Statements* (New York: American Institute of Certificated Public Accountants, October 1973), pp. 53–55.

10. National Association of Accountants, "Report of the Committee on Accounting for Corporate Social Performance," *Management Accounting* (February 1974), pp. 16–41.

11. A. Belkaoui, "The Accounting Treatments of Pollution Costs," *The Certificated General Accountant* (August 1973), pp. 19–21.

12. R. Ackerman, "How Companies Respond to Social Demands," *Harvard Business Review* (July–August 1973), pp. 88–98.

13. D. Beresford, *Compilation of Social Measurement Disclosure in Fortune 500 Annual Reports* (New York: Ernst & Ernst, 1973).

14. T. R. Dyckman, M. Gibbins, and R. J. Swieringa, "The Impact of Experimental and Survey Research," in A. R. Abdel-Khalik and T. F. Keller, eds., *The Impact of Accounting Research on Practice and Disclosure* (Durham, N.C.: Duke University Press, 1978).

15. A. Belkaoui, "Linguistic Relativity in Accounting," *Accounting, Organizations and Society* 3, no. 2 (1978), pp. 97–104.

16. A. Belkaoui, "The Interprofessional Linguistic Communication of Accounting Concepts: An Experiment in Sociolinguistics," *Journal of Accounting Research* (Fall 1980), pp. 362–376.

17. N. Tribhowan Jain, "Alternative Methods of Accounting and Decision Making: A Psycholinguistic Analysis," *The Accounting Review* (January 1973), pp. 95–104.

18. A. Belkaoui and Alain Consineau, "Accounting Information, Nonaccounting Information, and Common Stock Perception," *The Journal of Business* (July 1977), pp. 334–342.

19. A. Belkaoui, "Linguistic Relativity in Accounting," *Accounting, Organizations and Society* 3, no. 2 (1978), pp. 97–104.

20. W. G. Lewellen, R. C. Lease, and G. C. Schlarbaum, "Patterns of Investment Strategy and Behavior among Individual Investors," *The Journal of Business* (July 1977), pp. 296–333.

21. M. E. Barrett, "Accounting for Intercorporate Investments: A Behavioral Field Study," in *Empirical Research in Accounting: Selected Studies 1971, Journal of Accounting Research* 9, Supplement (1971), pp. 50–92.

22. Ralph W. Estes, "Socio-Economic Accounting and External Diseconomies," *The Accounting Review* (April 1972), pp. 284–290.

23. *Annual McGraw-Hill Survey of Pollution Control Expenditures* (New York: McGraw-Hill, 1970).

24. G. Bylinski, "The Mounting Bill for Pollution Control," *Fortune* (July 1971), p. 130.

25. W. G. Lewellen, R. C. Lease, and G. C. Schlarbaum, "Patterns of Investment Strategy and Behavior among Individual Investors," *The Journal of Business* (July 1977), pp. 296–333.

## SELECTED READINGS

Abdel-Khalik, A. R. "The Effect of Aggregating Accounting Reports on the Quality of the Lending Decision: An Empirical Investigation." *Empirical Research in Accounting: Selected Studies* (1973), pp. 104–138.

Ackerman, R. "How Companies Respond to Social Demands." *Harvard Business Review* (July–August 1973), pp. 88–98.

American Accounting Association, Committee on Accounting for Social Performance. "Report of the Committee on Accounting for Social Performance." *The Accounting Review* LI, Supplement (1976), 116–125.

American Accounting Association, Committee on Environment Effects of Organizational Behavior. "Report of the Committee on Environment Effects of Organizational Behavior." *The Accounting Review* XLIII, Supplement (1973), pp. 73–119.

American Accounting Association, Committee on Measurement of Social Costs. "Report of the Committee on Measurement of Social Costs." *The Accounting Review* XLIX, Supplement (1974), pp. 98–113.

American Accounting Association, Committee on Measures of Effectiveness for Social Programs. "Report of the Committee on Measures of Effectiveness for Social Programs." *The Accounting Review* XLVII, Supplement (1972), pp. 336–396.

American Accounting Association, Committee on Nonfinancial Measures of Ef-
    fectiveness. "Report of the Committee on Nonfinancial Measures of Ef-
    fectiveness." *The Accounting Review* XLV, Supplement (1971),
    pp. 164–211.
American Accounting Association, Committee on Social Costs. "Report of the
    Committee on Social Costs." *The Accounting Review* XLX, Supplement
    (1975), pp. 50–89.
American Institute of Certificated Public Accountants. "Report of the Study
    Group on the Objectives of Financial Statements." In *Objectives of Fi-
    nancial Statements*. New York: American Institute of Certificated Public
    Accountants, 1973.
*Annual McGraw-Hill Survey of Pollution Control Expenditures*. New York:
    McGraw-Hill, 1970.
Barrett, M. E. "Accounting for Intercorporate Investments: A Behavioral Field
    Study." *Empirical Research in Accounting: Selected Studies 1971. Jour-
    nal of Accounting Research* 9, Supplement (1971), pp. 50–92.
Beams, F. A., and Paul E. Fertig. "Pollution Control through Social Cost Con-
    version." *The Journal of Accounting* (November 1971), pp. 37–42.
Belkaoui, A. "The Accounting Treatments of Pollution Costs." *The Certificated
    General Accountant* (August 1973), pp. 19–21.
———. "The Impact of the Disclosure of the Environment Effects of Organi-
    zational Behavior on the Market." *Financial Management* (Winter
    1976), pp. 26–31.
———. "The Interprofessional Linguistic Communication of Accounting Con-
    cepts: An Experiment in Sociolinguistics." *Journal of Accounting Re-
    search* (Fall 1980), pp. 362–374.
———. "Linguistic Relativity in Accounting." *Accounting, Organizations and
    Society* 3, no. 2 (1978), pp. 97–104.
———. "The Whys and Wherefores of Measuring Externalities." *The Certifi-
    cated General Accountant* (January 1975), pp. 29–32.
Belkaoui, A. and Alain Consineau. "Accounting Information, Nonaccounting
    Information, and Common Stock Perception." *The Journal of Business*
    (July 1977), pp. 334–342.
Beresford, D. *Compilation of Social Measurement Disclosure in Fortune 500
    Annual Reports*. New York: Ernst & Ernst, 1973.
Bowman, Edward H. "Corporate Social Responsibility and the Investor." *Jour-
    nal of Contemporary Business* (Winter 1973), pp. 62–73.
Bragdon, Joseph H., Jr., and John Marlin. "Is Pollution Profitable? *Risk Man-
    agement* (April 1972), pp. 14–32.
Bruns, W., Jr. "Inventory Valuation and Management Decisions." *The Ac-
    counting Review* (April 1965), pp. 345–357.
Bylinski, G. "The Mounting Bill for Pollution Control." *Fortune* (July 1971),
    p. 130.

Dopuch, N., and J. Ronen, "The Effects of Alternative Inventory Valuation Methods—An Experimental Study." *Journal of Accounting Research* (Autumn 1973), pp. 191–211.

Dyckman, T. R. "The Effects of Alternative Accounting Techniques on Certain Management Decisions." *Journal of Accounting Research* (Spring 1964), pp. 91–107.

———. "On the Effects of Earnings—Trend, Size and Inventory Valuation Procedures in Evaluating a Business Firm." In R. Jaedicke, Y. Ijiri, and O. Nielson, eds. *Research in Accounting Measurement*. Evanston, Ill.: American Accounting Association, 1966, pp. 175–185.

Dyckman, T. R., M. Gibbins, and R. J. Swieringa. "The Impact of Experimental and Survey Research." In A. R. Abdel-Khalik and T. F. Keller, eds., *The Impact of Accounting Research on Practice and Disclosure*. Durham, N.C.: Duke University Press, 1978.

Elias, N. "The Effects of Human Asset Statements on the Investment Decision: An Experiment." *Empirical Research in Accounting: Selected Studies* (1972), pp. 241–266.

Estes, Ralph W. "Socio-Economic Accounting and External Diseconomies." *The Accounting Review* (April 1972), pp. 289–290.

Flamholtz, E., and E. Cook, "Connotative Meaning and Its Role in Accounting Change: A Field Study." *Accounting, Organizations and Society* (October 1978), pp. 115–140.

Haried, A. "Measurement of Meaning in Financial Reports." *Journal of Accounting Research* (Spring 1972), pp. 117–145.

———. "The Semantic Dimensions of Financial Reports." *Journal of Accounting Research* (Autumn 1973), pp. 376–391.

Hendricks, J. "The Impact of Human Resource Accounting Information on Stock Investment Decisions: An Empirical Study." *The Accounting Review* (April 1976), pp. 292–305.

Hofstedt, T. R. "Some Behavioral Parameters of Financial Analysis." *The Accounting Review* (October 1972), pp. 679–692.

Jain, Tribhowan N. "Alternative Methods of Accounting and Decision Making: A Psycholinguistic Analysis." *The Accounting Review* (January 1973), pp. 95–104.

Jensen, R. "An Experimental Design for the Study of Effects of Accounting Variations in Decision Making." *Journal of Accounting Research* (Autumn 1966), pp. 224–238.

Lewellen, W. G., R. C. Lease, and G. C. Schlarbaum. "Patterns of Investment Strategy and Behavior among Individual Investors." *The Journal of Business* (July 1977), pp. 296–333.

Livingstone, J. L. "A Behavioral Study of Tax Allocation in Electric Utility Regulations." *The Accounting Review* (July 1967), pp. 544–552.

Longstreth, B., and H. David Rosenblom. *Social Responsibility and the Institutional Investor*. New York: Praeger, 1973.

National Association of Accountants. "Report of the Committee on Accounting for Corporate Social Performance." *Management Accounting* (February 1974), pp. 16–41.

Oliver, B. "The Semantic Differential: A Device for Measuring the Interprofessional Communications of Selected Accounting Concepts." *Journal of Accounting Research* (Autumn 1974), pp. 299–316.

Ortman, R. F. "The Effects on Investment Analysis of Alternative Reporting Procedure for Diversified Firms." *The Accounting Review* (April 1975), pp. 298–304.

*Report of the Study Group on Objectives of Financial Statements*. New York: American Institute of Certificated Public Accountants, October 1973.

Siegel, S. *Nonparametric Statistics for the Behavioral Sciences*. New York: McGraw-Hill, 1956.

Simon, J. G., C. W. Pavers, and J. P. Gunnemann. *The Ethical Investor*. New Haven, Conn.: Yale University Press, 1972.

Spicer, Barry H. "Investors, Corporate Social Performance and Information Disclosure: An Empirical Study." *The Accounting Review* (January 1978), pp. 34–111.

Tukey, J. W. "One Degree of Freedom for Nonadditivity." *Biometrics* 5 (1949), pp. 232–242.

Winer, B. J. *Statistical Principles in Experimental Design* 2nd ed. New York: McGraw-Hill, 1971.

# 8

## Financial Outcomes of Socio-Economic Accounting: The Market Reaction to Socio-Economic Accounting Information

### INTRODUCTION[1]

Much of the debate accompanying America's social upheaval of recent years has concerned those actions of business firms that have had harmful effects on others. Called "externalities," these effects arise from the divergences between social and private costs of the firm. A major point of the debate is the absence in the firm's financial statements of information related to these externalities.

> The accounting profession, which sets the rules by which companies report their financial results, have so far taken no steps to require socially related data in routine corporate reports.[2]

While the accounting profession did not take positive steps in reporting separately such expenditures in the annual reports, we find that in 1970–1971 diverse companies in the chemical, food, pulp and paper, petroleum, and other industries included, either in the president's letters or in the review of operations, substantial information concerning pollution control expenditures.

The question is to know the usefulness of this disclosure in terms of its impact or effect, if any, on decision makers in the investment community. This effect, if any, is measured by observing the possible reaction of the stock market to the disclosure of such "social information," related specifically to pollution costs.

The aim of this chapter is

(a) to present the findings of a study investigating the association between profitability and pollution expenditures;

(b) to present the findings of another study investigating the reaction of the stock prices of fifty companies subsequent to the disclosure by these companies of pollution control expenditures in their 1970s annual reports.

## ASSOCIATION BETWEEN PROFITABILITY AND POLLUTION CONTROL EXPENDITURES

### Problem

A study by Bragdon and Martin[3] was designed to test the negative hypothesis that social responsibility is necessarily unprofitable, that is, the hypothesis that firms in the pulp and paper industry that have good records in installing antipollution equipment have been the least profitable. Bragdon and Martin found, however, that the hypothesis was untenable and that a good pollution record is associated with high profits. They did so by comparing the earnings-per-share growth of seventeen pulp and paper companies between 1965 and 1970 and their indicators of pollution control adequacy measured by three indices derived from the Council Economic Priorities study on the pulp and paper industry. The first two indices represent the percentage of plants operated by a firm that has an adequate degree of pollution control; the third index is a number (1, 2, or 3, signifying good, average, or poor, respectively), indicating the Council of Economic Priorities' evaluation of a company's overall performance in pollution control. The choice of a qualitative index as an independent variable puts some limitations on the validity of their study. It would be more appropriate to test the possible association between the pollution expenditures in dollar amounts and the earnings per share. Hence, in this study it is intended to test the degree of association between

(a) the ratio of pollution expenditures over sales and earnings per share for the same firms in the pulp and paper industry, and

(b) the ratio of pollution expenditures over capital expenditures and earnings per share for the above firms.

The choice of the ratios of pollution expenditures over sales and that over capital expenditures as measures of the variable in our study is motivated by the general belief that pollution expenditures, as a rule of thumb, will be a function of the sales amount or the capital expenditure amount.

The hypotheses to be tested will be:

$H_1$:   There is no association between the ratio of pollution expenditures over sales and earnings per share for the firms investigated.

$H_2$:   There is no association between the ratio of pollution expenditures over capital expenditures and earnings per share for the firms investigated.

## Methodology

1. The average of the yearly ratio of pollution expenditures over sales between 1965 and 1970 was computed for thirteen firms in the pulp and paper industry (Exhibit 8.1).

2. The average of the yearly ratio of pollution expenditures over capital expenditures between 1965 and 1970 was computed for the same thirteen firms (Exhibit 8.2).

3. The dependent variable, profitability, is measured as the average earnings growth during 1965–1970.

4. The degree of association between the two variables will be measured using the Spearman's coefficient of rank correlation.

## Results and Interpretation

Exhibits 8.1, 8.2, and 8.3 show the results. The coefficient between the ratio of pollution expenditures to sales and earnings per share for the period 1965–1970 was found to be significant at the 1 percent confidence level. The coefficient between the ratio of pollution expenditures to capital expenditures for the same period was also found to be significant at

Exhibit 8.1
Companies Investigated in the Pulp and Paper Industry

| Paper Company | | Pollution Expenditures (Sales for 1965–1970) | Pollution Expenditures (Capital Exp. for 1965–1970) | Earnings per Share Growth for 1965–1970 | Average Return on Capital 1965–1970 | Average Return on Equity 1965–1970 | Earnings Net Worth 1970 |
|---|---|---|---|---|---|---|---|
| Weyerhauser | 1 | 2.10% | 10.0% | 9.4% | 11.70% | 13.7% | 1.28% |
| Georgia Pacific | 2 | 0.60 | 3.0 | 5.7 | 8.30 | 15.8 | 1.40 |
| Union Camp | 3 | 0.49 | 2.9 | 5.0 | 8.80 | 12.2 | 0.73 |
| Owens Illinois | 4 | 0.25 | 2.0 | 3.9 | 7.00 | 11.6 | 0.066 |
| Diamond International | 5 | — | — | 2.3 | 13.10 | 15.0 | 0.25 |
| International Paper | 6 | 0.30 | 3.0 | 1.4 | 8.70 | 9.6 | 0.56 |
| Kimberly Clark | 7 | 0.31 | 3.1 | 0.9 | 9.50 | 7.9 | 0.91 |
| Scott | 8 | 0.31 | 3.2 | 0.9 | 9.40 | 11.6 | 0.75 |
| St. Regis | 9 | 0.26 | 3.4 | 0.4 | 6.10 | 7.6 | 0.45 |
| Hammermill | 10 | 0.58 | 3.0 | −2.3 | 7.20 | 10.2 | 0.50 |
| Westvale | 11 | 0.22 | 1.8 | −2.4 | 6.70 | 9.2 | 0.63 |
| Boise Cascade | 12 | 0.19 | 2.1 | −3.1 | NA | NA | NA |
| U.S. Plywood Champ | 13 | 0.40 | 7.0 | −10.7 | 5.60 | 6.9 | 2.09 |

**Exhibit 8.2**
**Pollution Expenditures/Capital Expenditures versus EPS Growth**

| Firm | Pollution Expenditures Capital Expenditures | Rank | EPS Growth | Rank | di | di2 |
|------|------|------|------|------|------|------|
| 1 | 10.0% | 1 | 9.4% | 1 | 0 | 0 |
| 2 | 3.0 | 5 | 5.7 | 2 | 3 | 9 |
| 3 | 2.9 | 8 | 5.0 | 3 | 5 | 25 |
| 4 | 2.0 | 10 | 3.9 | 4 | 6 | 36 |
| 5 | — | — | 2.3 | — | — | — |
| 6 | 3.0 | 7 | 1.4 | 5 | 2 | 4 |
| 7 | 3.1 | 4 | 0.9 | 6.5 | − 2.5 | 6.25 |
| 8 | 3.2 | 3 | 0.9 | 6.5 | − 3.5 | 12.25 |
| 9 | 3.4 | 2 | 0.4 | 8 | 6 | 36 |
| 10 | 3.0 | 6 | − 2.3 | 9 | 3 | 9 |
| 11 | 1.8 | 11 | − 2.4 | 10 | 1 | 1 |
| 12 | 2.1 | 9 | − 3.1 | 11 | − 2 | 4 |
| 13 | — | — | — | — | — | — |

$R_s = 0.36$, $t = 3.267$, significant at 0.01 level

the 1 percent confidence level. It could be deduced from both results that in the pulp and paper industry there is an association between profitability and pollution control policies, and that the firms in the pulp and paper industry that have good records in installing pollution control equipment are the most profitable. However, one might argue that it is the firms with the most profits that have the most to spend on pollution control. This reaction does not fit the circumstances of the industry, where two of the pollution control leaders have been involved in this activity since the 1940s when they were not profit leaders. Then an interpretation of the results could be made in terms of lower operating and financial costs and higher revenues.[4]

Hence, operating costs might have been reduced because of pollution control in the following ways:

a. Labor costs are lower because of better health conditions.

b. Committed costs, as for insurance, are lower.

c. Taxation is lower because of a federal tax write-off provision for pollution control equipment.

d. Legal costs are lower.

**Exhibit 8.3**
**Comparison between Pollution Expenditures/Sales and EPS Growth**

| Firm | Pollution Expenditures Sales | Rank | EPS Growth | Rank | di | di2 |
|------|------|------|------|------|------|------|
| 1 | 2.1% | 1 | 9.4% | 1 | 0 | 0 |
| 2 | 0.60 | 2 | 5.7 | 2 | 0 | 0 |
| 3 | 0.49 | 4 | 5.0 | 3 | 1 | 1 |
| 4 | 0.25 | 9 | 3.9 | 4 | 3 | 9 |
| 5 | — | — | — | — | — | — |
| 6 | 0.30 | 7 | 1.4 | 5 | 2 | 4 |
| 7 | 0.31 | 5.5 | 0.9 | 6.5 | 1 | 1 |
| 8 | 0.31 | 5.5 | 0.9 | 6.5 | 1 | 1 |
| 9 | 0.26 | 8 | 0.4 | 8 | 0 | 0 |
| 10 | 0.58 | 3 | −2.3 | 9 | 6 | 12 |
| 11 | 0.22 | 10 | −2.4 | 10 | 0 | 0 |
| 12 | 0.19 | 11 | −3.1 | 11 | 0 | 0 |
| 13 | — | — | — | — | — | — |

$R_s = 0.88$, $t = 5.890$, significant at 0.01 level

In addition to operating costs, financial costs will be lowered because of the new image and the possibility of easily raising additional capital. Revenue might get higher than the involvement of pollution-control-conscious customers.

### Conclusions

The association between profitability and pollution control is admitted based on evidence from the pulp and paper industry. Other things being equal, the disclosure of such expenditures might affect the market. Any market response to the disclosure, if any, should show up in a large sample of fifty companies. Thus the major question to be asked in the next section is as follows: Did the disclosure of pollution control expenditure by a company have any impact on the stock market behavior of its stocks?

## STOCK MARKET REACTION TO ENVIRONMENTAL ACCOUNTING

Corporations interact with their environment. Guiding their behavior is the goal of maximizing shareholder wealth, an objective that is not obviously affected by social costs associated with pollution and other externalities.[5] These social costs should be identified, measured, and reported if corporations are to fulfill their social as well as their shareholder responsibilities.[6]

The accounting profession has taken few positive steps to report social costs and the expenditures made by corporations to reduce them. However, the 1970–1971 annual reports of companies in industries as diverse as chemical, food, petroleum, and pulp and paper do include information on pollution control either in the president's letter or in the review of operations. This disclosure suggests that the managers of some corporations see an advantage in making these expenditures and see some reason for disclosing that information to investors.

The pollution abatement expenditures are not trivial. For some large firms they may reach 4 percent of sales and 10 percent of capital investment.[7] In the steel industry, the abatement costs are reported to be as high as 25 percent of capital investment. Their size supports the conclusion that these expenditures provide material information to investors. The information is essential if investors are going to properly consider the negative effects of pollution abatement expenditures on earnings per share along with any compensating, positive effects that reduce risk or create greater interest from a particular investment clientele.

Some argue that risk-reducing effects will more than compensate for expenditures on pollution control: "Between firms competing in the capital markets those perceived to have the highest expected future earnings in combination with the lowest expected risk from environmental and other factors will be most successful at attracting long-term funds."[8] Others believe that "ethical investors" form a clientele that responds to demonstrations of corporate social concern.[9] Investors of this type would like to avoid particular investments entirely for ethical reasons, as the 1966–1968 Committee on External Reporting of the American Accounting Association points out, and would prefer to favor socially responsible corporations in their portfolios. The United Church of Christ, for example, has issued a sixty-one-page booklet, *Investing Church Funds for Maximum Social Impact*, which advises investment in socially responsible firms. A different view is summed up in the Beams-Fertig theory,[10] which holds that corporations that report the least activity in avoiding social cost will appear more successful to investors and will be favored by the market.

These conflicting views on the effect of pollution control expenditures and their disclosure provide two hypotheses about stock price behavior:

1. During the months following the disclosure date of pollution control expenditures (annual report date), the common stock prices of disclosing corporations will be favorably affected.

2. Corporations identical in asset size and industry classification that do not disclose such expenditures will not be as favorably affected.

Acceptance of both hypotheses is equivalent to refuting the view that corporations demonstrating and reporting the least concern for social costs are rewarded by the capital market.

## THEORETICAL JUSTIFICATION

Two competing theories explain the impact of pollution control expenditures on the stock market.

The first is an efficient market view. Pollution control expenditures affect earnings per share directly by increasing the cost of the goods sold and indirectly by affecting the expected risk from environmental factors. The net result could be a decrease in earnings per share and a reduced risk. In short, the disclosure of such expenditure might be followed by both a change in expected earnings and a change in risk class and discount rate. The market would react to the information content of disclosure. Such a reaction is consistent with the proposition that the market for securities is a semistrong efficient market in the sense that market prices "fully reflect" all publicly available information, and, by implication, that market prices react instantaneously and without bias to new information. In the semistrong hypothesis of an efficient market, pollution control expenditures would constitute "inside information" and there should be no market reaction until they become public information in the financial statements. If reactions occur after disclosure, then it can be concluded that disclosure of abatement costs reflects events that affect the value of a corporation.

The second view, often referred to as the "naïve investor hypothesis," assumes that the majority of investors are relatively unsophisticated with respect to accounting techniques. These investors regard changes in earnings per share more important and consequently do not react to specific information such as pollution control expenditures. They are conditioned to react to accounting data only in terms of earnings per share. As stated by Sterling: "Accounting reports have been issued for a long time, and their issuance has been accompanied by a rather impressive ceremony performed by the managers and accountants who issue them. The receivers are likely to have gained the impression that they ought to react, and have noted that others react, and thereby have become conditioned to react."[11]

With these opposing theories and the objectives of the study in mind, two groups of fifty American firms from different industries were chosen. The first, an experimental group, included those firms that disclosed pollution control information in their 1970 annual reports. An attempt was made to choose firms with material pollution control expense equivalent to at least 1 percent of their sales. The second, a control group, included firms of a similar industrial classification and asset size (see Exhibit 8.4).

## EXPERIMENTAL VARIABLE

The market model was used. It defines the stochastic process generating security price changes.

$$r_{it} = \alpha_i + \beta r_{mt} + U_{it}$$

where:

$r_{it}$ = continuously compounded rate of return of security $i$ in period $t$
   $= \text{Ln} (1 + R_{it}) = \text{Ln} [(P_t + D_t)/P_{t-1}]$,

$R_{it}$ = noncompounded single-period return of security $i$ in period $t$,

$\alpha_i, \beta_i$ = intercept and slope of the linear relationship between $r_{it}$ and $r_{mt}$,

$r_{mt}$ = market factor in period $t$
   $= \text{Ln} (\text{sp500}_t/\text{sp500}_{t-1})$, and

$U_{it}$ = stochastic portion of individualistic component of $r_{it}$.

In this model, $r_{it}$ is used instead of $R_{it}$ because it has fewer outliers in its relative frequency distribution and will therefore yield more efficient risk statistics than $R_{it}$. Also, it is distributed more symmetrically than the positively skewed $V$ variable.

This model basically shows the existing linear relationship between the expected return on security $i$ and the expected return of the market factor represented here by the Standard and Poor 500. The rationale for such a model is the ability to discriminate between two types of events that affect a security's return: the market events that cause a response

# Exhibit 8.4
## Investigated Companies Disclosing Pollution Control Expenditures in 1970s Annual Reports

| Experimental Group | Control Group |
|---|---|
| 1. Alleghay Ludlum Inds | 1. Wheeling Pittsburgh Steel |
| 2. Allied Chemical Corp. | 2. American Cyanamid Co. |
| 3. American Metal Climax, Inc. | 3. International Mineral Chemical |
| 4. American Seating Co. | 4. Cleveland Cliffs Iron Co. |
| 5. American Smelting and Refining | 5. Foote Mineral Co. |
| 6. Anaconda Co. | 6. Kennecott Copper Co. |
| 7. Armco Steel Corp. | 7. Inland Steel Co. |
| 8. Atlantic Richfield Co. | 8. Skelly Oil Co. |
| 9. Bemis Co. | 9. Reynolds Metal |
| 10. Bethlehem Steel Corp. | 10. U.S. Steel Co. |
| 11. Bucyrus Erie Co. | 11. Massey Ferguson |
| 12. Celanese Corp. | 12. Fedders Corp. |
| 13. Continental Can Co., Inc. | 13. Olin Corp. |
| 14. Continental Oil Co. | 14. National Can Corp. |
| 15. Copperweld Steel | 15. Getty Oil Co. |
| 16. Deere Co. | 16. Continental Copper & Steel Ind. |
| 17. Dow Chemical | 17. Caterpillar Tractor Co. |
| 18. E. I. DuPont de Nemours | 18. Monsanto Co. |
| 19. Eastman Kodak Co. | 19. Union Carbide Corp. |
| 20. Ford Motor Co. | 20. Uniroyal, Inc. |
| 21. General Foods Corp. | 21. Chrysler Corp. |
| 22. Georgia Pacific Corp. | 22. Kellogg Co. |
| 23. Gerber Products Co. | 23. Evans Products Co. |
| 24. B. F. Goodrich Co. | 24. Quaker Oats Co. |
| 25. Hercules, Inc. | 25. Goodyear Tire & Rubber Co. |
| 26. International Paper Co. | 26. Alcan Aluminum |
| 27. Walter Kiddle Co. | 27. Granite City Steel |
| 28. Mobil Oil Corp. | 28. Kimberley Clark |
| 29. Marcor, Inc. | 29. Stauffer Chemical Co. |
| 30. National Cash Register Co. | 30. Quaker State Oil Ref. |
| 31. Owens Illinois, Inc. | 31. CCI Corporation |
| 32. Penwalt Corp. | 32. Xerox |
| 33. Phelps Dodge Corp. | 33. Crown Zellerbach |
| 34. Philips Petroleum Co. | 34. Burrough Corp. |
| 35. Dart Industries | 35. Grandly Mining |
| 36. St. Regis Paper Co. | 36. Clark Oil & Refining Co. |
| 37. Scott Paper Co. | 37. Hammermill Paper Co. |
| 38. Shell Oil Co. | 38. Great Northern Nekoosa Corp. |
| 39. Standard Oil of California | 39. Royal Dutch Petroleum Co. |
| 40. Standard Oil of Indiana | 40. Texaco Inc. |
| 41. Time Inc. | 41. Gulf Oil Corp. |
| 42. Union Camp Corp. | 42. McGraw-Hill Inc. |
| 43. U.S. Plywood Champ Papers | 43. Westvaco Corp. |
| 44. Weyerhauser Co. | 44. American Can Co. |
| 45. White Motors Corp. | 45. Carborundum Co. |
| 46. Boise Cascade Corp. | 46. Cummins Engine |
| 47. Diamond Shamrock Corp. | 47. Mead Corporation |
| 48. I.T.T. Corp. | 48. Brown Co. |
| 49. Diamond International Corp. | 49. General Electric |
| 50. Interlake Steel | 50. Riegel Paper |

*Source*: Ahmed Belkaoui, "The Impact of the Disclosure of the Environmental Effects of Organizational Behavior on the Market," *Financial Management* 5, no. 4 (Winter 1976), p. 31. Reprinted with permission from Financial Management Association International, College of Business Administration #3331, University of South Florida, Tampa, FL 33620–5500, (813) 974–2084.

reflected in $\beta_i$ and the events particular to security $i$, which are reflected by the residual $U_{it}$. The error term $U_{it}$ is the portion of security return not attributable to general economic effects. In this study, the isolation of these two types of events is essential for testing the information effect of pollution control expenditures.

## DATA COLLECTION, REGRESSION ESTIMATION, AND ERROR TERMS

The precise month $T$ in which the pollution control information reached the market was determined from the annual report disclosing the pollution control information. Then, monthly closing common stock prices were obtained for each of the 100 companies for the 12 months before and 12 months after the annual report announcement. The Standard and Poor 500 for the same months was used as the general market index of performance. Both stock price and Standard and Poor relatives were recorded each month from $T - 12$ to $T + 12$, a total of 24 observations, for each company. The parameters of the market model $\alpha_i$ and $\beta_i$ were determined for each company by a least square regression over the 24 observations. On the basis of the above results, the error term $U_{it}$ for each company and for each of the 24 months was computed as follows:

$$U_{it} = r_{it} - \alpha_i - \beta_i \, r_{mt}$$

These errors, as stated earlier, impound all the factors influencing the company that are independent of market events. To abstract the general trend due to the disclosure impact from the individual company fluctuations, an average residual across companies for each period and for both the experimental and control groups was computed as follows:

$$\bar{U}_t = \sum \bar{U}_t / N$$

where

$N = 50$ companies per group.

These $\bar{U}_t$'s can be interpreted as the average percentage deviations of the returns of surveyed companies from the general stock market movements. They are the data used in testing this study's hypotheses.

**Exhibit 8.5**
**Average Residual Errors**

| Time Intervals | Experimental Group Average Residuals | Experimental Group Standard Deviation | Control Group Average Residuals | Control Group Standard Deviation |
|---|---|---|---|---|
| T−12 | −0.05303 | 0.2890 | −0.02096 | 0.2342 |
| T−11 | −0.06501 | 0.3820 | −0.08290 | 0.3292 |
| T−10 | −0.07420 | 0.3030 | −0.04462 | 0.3131 |
| T−9 | −0.08261 | 0.2670 | −0.06360 | 0.2271 |
| T−8 | −0.02605 | 0.2842 | −0.02161 | 0.2868 |
| T−7 | −0.07341 | 0.3230 | −0.02001 | 0.5160 |
| T−6 | −0.09735 | 0.4390 | +0.01252 | 0.3696 |
| T−5 | −0.05231 | 0.2781 | +0.06237 | 0.3250 |
| T−4 | −0.04211 | 0.5932 | +0.08011 | 0.3393 |
| T−3 | −0.08123 | 0.3620 | +0.15601 | 0.6201 |
| T−2 | −0.02811 | 1.0031 | +0.13351 | 0.5930 |
| T−1 | −0.01739 | 0.5632 | +0.15450 | 0.6031 |
| T+1 | +0.11201 | 0.2231 | +0.15230 | 0.3120 |
| T+2 | +0.12362 | 0.3681 | +0.15031 | 0.2231 |
| T+3 | +0.06471 | 0.4340 | +0.03337 | 0.5322 |
| T+4 | +0.02133 | 0.9091 | +0.02302 | 0.6631 |
| T+5 | −0.01020 | 0.2120 | −0.05321 | 0.2121 |
| T+6 | −0.01899 | 0.4230 | −0.03231 | 0.5260 |
| T+7 | −0.02261 | 0.6230 | −0.04360 | 0.3121 |
| T+8 | −0.04150 | 0.5210 | −0.02020 | 0.2191 |
| T+9 | −0.04360 | 0.2021 | −0.04262 | 0.2222 |
| T+10 | −0.06135 | 0.2320 | −0.05781 | 0.2172 |
| T+11 | −0.04241 | 0.3121 | −0.05374 | 0.6320 |
| T+12 | −0.02181 | 0.3323 | −0.08120 | 0.6132 |

*Source*: Ahmed Belkaoui, "The Impact of the Disclosure of the Environmental Effects of Organizational Behavior on the Market," *Financial Management* 5, no. 4 (Winter 1976), p. 28. Reprinted with permission from Financial Management Association International, College of Business Administration #3331, University of South Florida, Tampa, FL 33620–5500, (813) 974–2084.

## DATA ANALYSIS AND INTERPRETATION

The error terms, $\bar{U}_t$, for each group from Exhibit 8.5 are plotted in Exhibit 8.6. For the experimental group, Exhibit 8.6 shows that most of the error terms prior to disclosure data are located in the lower left quadrant while four of the error terms subsequent to the disclosure data are positive and located in the upper right quadrant, and the rest of the errors are negative and in the lower right quadrant. The same exhibit shows a behavior of the error terms for the control group completely different from that of the experimental group. The Mann-Whitney test was applied to the error data. Like other nonparametric tests, it does not require rigid assumptions about the population from which samples are

**Exhibit 8.6**
**Plot of Average Errors**

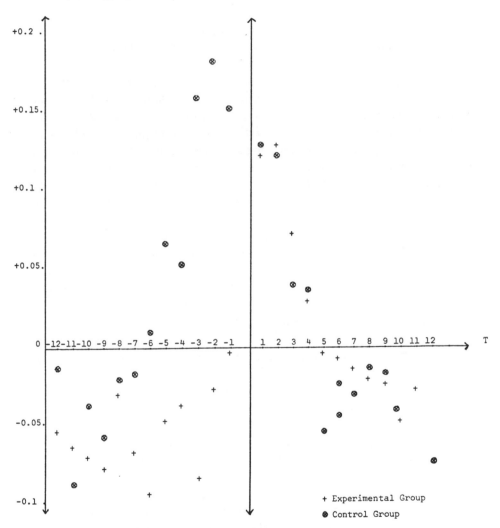

*Source*: Ahmed Belkaoui, "The Impact of the Disclosure of the Environmental Effects of Organizational Behavior on the Market," *Financial Management* 5, no. 4 (Winter 1976), p. 29. Reprinted with permission from Financial Management Association International, College of Business Administration #3331, University of South Florida, Tampa, FL 33620–5500, (813) 974–2084.

taken.[12] The first null hypothesis was that the experimental group and the control group had the same distribution. The second null hypothesis was that error terms for the experimental group had the same distribution before and after the disclosure date. Both hypotheses were rejected in a two-tail test at $\alpha = 0.002$.

The results can be interpreted considering both the efficient market hypothesis and the naïve investor hypothesis. During the period prior to disclosure of pollution control expenditures, the disclosing companies were performing more poorly than the market. For a period of four months after disclosure the performance of the stocks was better than market, indicating a sharp reaction to disclosure. The advantage over the market decreased from $T + 2$ to $T + 4$ and then became a disadvantage for the rest of the period, implying that the additional information had an immediate, but temporary effect on the market. The first explanation would be that the market made a temporary conversion of the positive effect of pollution control expenditures in higher share valuation. This raised the price of the group to a level where the efficient market found them to be fully valued and started selling the shares. This led prices to go down to a level where the market appraised them on fundamentals. The results, accordingly, follow the "efficient market hypothesis" over a wide period of time. The second explanation would be that the increase in the market price takes place when "ethical" investors buy shares on the strength of better social image conveyed by the disclosure. However, such predisposition was only temporary, as conveyed by the decrease from $T + 2$. In this respect the results follow the "naïve investor hypothesis" over a short period of time.

## CONCLUSION

It is evidently quite difficult to isolate the specific effects of pollution control expenditures on the price behavior of the stock market because of the presence of a myriad of other influencing factors. This investigation of fifty companies that disclosed their pollution control expenditures showed a significant change centered on the date of disclosure, and the resulting expectations had apparently a substantial and temporary effect on the stock market performance. This result follows the efficient market hypothesis in its semistrong form. Under the naïve investor hypothesis it verifies the existence of an "ethical investor." In general, this study refutes the suggestion that the worst offenders in the reporting of social costs will be rewarded more in the capital market. In fact, on the basis of these results, managers may be advised to allocate a proportion of their resources to pollution control and to report these expenditures to the stockholders. One might even assume that in the long run, the firm that installs pollution control devices now may have better income and less risk of plant closings by the Environmental Protection Agency in the next decade than a competing firm that postpones such expenditures until it is forced to make them later.

## NOTES

1. Parts of this chapter have been adapted from Ahmed Belkaoui, "The Impact of the Disclosure of the Environment Effects of Organizational Behavior on the Market," *Financial Management* 5, no. 4 (Winter 1976), pp. 26–31. Reprinted with permission from Financial Management Association International, College of Business Administration #3331, University of South Florida, Tampa, FL 33620-5500, (813) 974-2084.

2. "The Arithmetic of Quality," *Wall Street Journal*, 9 December 1971, p. 71.

3. Joseph H. Bragdon and John A. Martin, "Pollution and Profitability: The Case of the Pulp and Paper Industry," *Proceedings of the Financial Management Association*, Denver, Colorado (October 1971), pp. 16–25.

4. Bragdon and Martin, "Pollution and Profitability," p. 120.

5. Ahmed Belkaoui, "The Whys and Wherefores of Measuring Externalities," *The Certified General Accountant* (January 1975), pp. 29–32.

6. Ahmed Belkaoui, "The Accounting Treatment of Pollution Costs," *The Certified General Accountant* (August 1973), pp. 19–21.

7. "Report of the Committee on Environmental Effects of Organizational Behavior," *The Accounting Review* XLVIII Supplement (1970), p. 88.

8. "Pollution Price Tag: 71 Billion Dollars," *U.S. News and World Report*, 17 August 1970, p. 41.

9. "Report of the Committee on External Reporting," *The Accounting Review* XLIV, Supplement (1969), p. 118.

10. Floyd A. Beams and Paul E. Fertig, "Pollution Control through Social Cost Conversion," *The Journal of Accounting* (November 1971), pp. 37–42.

11. Robert Sterling, "On Theory Construction and Verification," *The Accounting Review* (July 1970), p. 453.

12. Sydney Siegel, *Non-Parametric Statistics for the Behavioral Sciences* (New York: McGraw-Hill, 1956), pp. 116–126.

## SELECTED READINGS

Beams, Floyd A., and Paul E. Fertig. "Pollution Control through Social Cost Conversion." *The Journal of Accounting* (November 1971), pp. 37–42.

Belkaoui, Ahmed. "The Accounting Treatment of Pollution Costs." *The Certified General Accountant* (August 1973), pp. 19–21.

———. "The Whys and Wherefores of Measuring Externalities." *The Certified General Accountant* (January 1975), pp. 29–32.

Bylinski, Gene. "The Mounting Bill for Pollution Control." *Fortune* (July 1971), p. 130.

Elton, E., and M. Gruber. "Portfolio Theory Where Investment Relatives Are Log-normally Distributed." *Journal of Finance* (September 1974), pp. 25–36.

Fama, E. F., L. Fisher, M. C. Jensen, and R. Roll. "The Adjustment of Stock Prices to New Information." *International Economic Review* (February 1969), pp. 1–21.

Francis, J. C. "Skewness and Investor Decision." *Journal of Financial and Quantitative Analysis* (March 1975), pp. 62–73.

Markowitz, Harry M. *Portfolio Selection, Efficient Diversification of Investments*. New York: Wiley, 1959.

"Pollution Price Tag: 71 Billion Dollars." *U.S. News and World Report*, 17 August 1970, p. 41.

"Report of the Committee on Environmental Effects of Organizational Behavior." *The Accounting Review* XLVIII Supplement (1970), p. 88.

"Report of the Committee on External Reporting." *The Accounting Review* XLIV, Supplement (1969), p. 118.

Sharpe, William F. "A Simplified Model for Portfolio Analysis." *Management Sciences* (January 1963), pp. 337–392.

Siegel, Sydney. *Non-Parametric Statistics for the Behavioral Sciences*. New York: McGraw-Hill, 1956.

Simon, John G., Charles W. Pavers, and John P. Gunnemann. *The Ethical Investor*. New Haven and London: Yale University Press, 1972.

Sterling, Robert. "On Theory Construction and Verification." *The Accounting Review* (July 1970), p. 453.

# 9

# Financial Outcomes of Socio-Economic Accounting: The Effects of Regulatory Costs and Level of Exposure to Environmental Risk on the Extent of Environmental Disclosure

## INTRODUCTION

Research on the social responsibility accounting of firms examining the various relationships between social disclosure, social performance, and economic performance has been conducted since the early sixties[1] and continues to be the subject of academic interest.[2-4] One line of research examined the potential relationships between the extensiveness of a firm's social disclosure and its social performance with the hypothesis that the quantity and quality of social disclosure is positively correlated with its social performance.[5-12] Different measures of social disclosure have been used, including: (a) a social disclosure scale derived, (b) the percentage of prose in annual reports, (c) the quality of disclosure in annual reports, and (d) the quantity of disclosure in annual reports. Similarly, social performance has been measured differently as based on content analysis including: (a) reputational scales using both word and page counts from *Business and Society Review*,[13] (b) Moskowitz[14] reputational scales, citizenship awards, (c) CEP pollution information index, and (d) a student evaluation of industry reputation. The results included no correlation in four studies, negative correlation in one study, and positive correlation in three studies. The results point to two major inconsistencies: (a) lack of theory, and (b) diversity of the empirical databases examined.

   This study corrects for both inconsistencies in examining the relationship between environmental disclosures resulting from environmental
legislation and the regulatory costs and size of the environmental exposure for a sample of fifty-one chemical firms. The choice of the independent variables rests on the discretionary disclosure and legitimacy
theses. The empirical data are based on information in 10-K reports and
EPA reports. The results of the study show that an environmental disclosure index, based on environmental information from the 10-K report,
is related positively to (a) an index of regulatory costs based on three
Environmental Protection Agency measures of Superfund costs and (b)
the logarithm of chemical revenues as a measure of the size of the environmental exposure.


## SUPERFUND LEGISLATION

   In 1980, Congress passed the Comprehensive Environmental Response
Compensation and Liability Act, which created the Superfund to pay for
cleanup and enforcement activities of hazardous waste sites. The act
allowed the federal government to recover costs from those responsible
for environmental pollution through "strict," "joint and several," and
"retroactive" liability provisions. On October 17, 1986, Congress enacted the Superfund Amendments and Reauthorization Act of 1986
(SARA) bringing four major changes to the Superfund Program. They
were (1) an increase in the trust fund from $1.6 billion to $9 billion over
five years, (2) the expansion of overall cleanup standards, (3) the provision of new enforcement authorities and settlement tools, and (4) the
enactment of new planning and annual reporting requirements for facil-
ities handling hazardous chemicals (with Title III of SARA, the Emer-
gency Planning and Community Right-to-Know Act [EPCRA] of 1986
[EPA 1991]). Both laws provided a new empirical database on environmental disclosures and regulatory costs.


## HYPOTHESES

### Relationship of Environmental Disclosures to
### Regulatory Costs

Environmental disclosures are a form of discretionary disclosures.
Two types of analytical models examined the rationale behind environmental disclosures. The first type implied that managers disclose only

*relatively* good news. Verrecchia[15] imposes a constant proprietary cost of disclosure and finds that only managers with news above a threshold level will disclose their news. Similarly, Dye[16] assumes that investors are not sure about the existence of managers' private information and therefore cannot infer from no disclosure that managers are reluctant to disclose bad news. Both models imply that firms disclose relatively good news. Thus, firms with relatively good "news" (i.e., less negative news) about their environmental efforts would have an incentive to include environmental disclosures proportional to their regulatory costs.

The second analytical model implies that managers use discretionary disclosure to affect the behavior of product-market competitors. Darrough and Stoughton[17] used a model to endogenize proprietary disclosure costs and show that the disclosure of bad news is intended to discourage entry. Dontoh's[18] model for firms in oligopolistic markets shows that managers are likely to disclose good news to stockholders and bad news to competitors. The same argument is made by Newman and Sansing[19] using models in which disclosure is not limited to truthful ones. Thus, chemical firms with relatively "bad news" about their regulatory costs would have an incentive to include proportional environmental disclosures that may affect the behavior of product-market competitors.

The hypothesis that may be derived from both discretionary disclosure models is as follows:

$H_1$:   Firms include environmental disclosures in proportion to their regulatory costs.

### Relationship of Environmental Disclosure to the Level of Exposure to Environmental Risk

Corporate legitimacy has been used as an argument both for and against the need for environmental disclosure.[20,21] Legitimacy based on a social contract between the firm and society may be viewed as market-based, thereby directing firms in social activities that are profit-oriented. It is also viewed as society-based in the sense that social and public pressures direct firms toward social responsibility. As a result, social disclosure in general, and environmental disclosure in particular, may be used as a response to society's demands for social responsibility. Basically, firms will use environmental disclosures as a cost-effective means of addressing the "exposure" of the firms to the social/political climate. The higher the level of exposure to environmental risk, the higher the environmental disclosure of firms. Assuming the level of exposure to environmental risk is best measured by the level of chemical revenues, the following hypothesis may be derived from the legitimacy thesis:

$H_2$:   Firms include environmental disclosures in proportion to the level of exposure to environmental risk as measured by the level of chemical revenues.

## EMPIRICAL ANALYSIS

### Sample Firms

To be included in the sample, a firm must meet the following criteria:

1. The firm has a two-digit SIC code of 28 ("Chemical and Allied Products") in COMPUSTAT or was identified as involved in chemical operations in such sources as *Chemical Week, Moody's Industrial Review, Standard and Poor's Industry Surveys, Chemicals, Forbes, Fortune*, and the *Wall Street Journal*.
2. The firm has available EPA Superfund data and 1984 financial reports.

Fifty-one firms met the two criteria. They are identified in Exhibit 9.1.

### Measurement of Environmental Disclosure

The measurement of environmental disclosure is best achieved by a clear identification of specific statements in the 10-K reports on the extent of the environmental concern of the firm. It requires an identification of the areas of environmental concern and an appropriate scoring of the level of environmental disclosure.

Each firm is rated on the number of areas of environmental concern it included in its 1984 10-K report. A score of one is given for each area presented or discussed in the report. The areas of environmental concern considered are:

1. Statements citing or discussing current or proposed regulations.
2. Statements on the compliance status or compliance efforts of the company relative to environmental standards.

**Exhibit 9.1**
**Sample of Firms**

Abbott Labs

Air Products & Chemicals

American Cyanamid

Amoco

Atlantic Richfield

Carter Wallace

CBI Industries

Celanese Corp.

Dexter Corp.

Dow Chemical

E. I. Du Pont de Nemours

Eastman Kodak

Engelhard Corp.

Ethyl Corp.

Ferro Corp.

First Mississippi

B. F. Goodrich

Goodyear

W. R. Grace & Co.

Grow Group Inc.

Guardsman Products

Hercules Inc.

Hexcel Corp.

International Flavor

L S B Industries Inc.

Lawter International

Loctite Corp.

Merck & Co.

Minnesota Mining & Mfg.

Monsanto Company

N L Industries

Nalco Chemical

Olin

P P G Industries

Pennwalt Corp.

Pfizer

Pratt & Lambert

Quantum Chemical

Reichhold Chemicals

Rhone-Poulenc Rorer

Rohm & Haas Co.

Schering Plough Corp.

Sherwin-Williams

Syntex Corp.

Union Camp Corp.

Unocal

Upjohn

Valspar Corp.

Vulcan Materials

Warner-Lambert

Witco Corp.

3. Presentation of current or past monetary expenditures relative to environmental standards.

4. Presentation of future estimates for monetary expenditures relative to environmental control.

5. Statements on current or potential environmental actions or lawsuits against the company (i.e., environmental litigation disclosures).

The scores range from one to five. Each report was evaluated by two independent reviewers given the potential for ambiguity in evaluating environmental disclosures using content analysis.

## Measurement of Regulatory Costs

Three alternative measures of the Superfund costs are used in this study. They are:

1. TCN: The cumulative number of Superfund Notice letters as of 1984.

2. TCRD: The total cost reported in the Records of Decisions as of 1984 across all sites for the firm.

3. TACR: The allocated cost reported in the Records of Decisions as of 1984 summed across all sites for the firm, based on an equal allocation.

The *Site Enforcement Tracking System*—a database of Superfund Notice Letters—is used for determination of the number of Superfund sites per firm through 1984. The *Records of Decisions Annual Reports*—a database of abstracts and decisions for specific Superfund sites—is used for determination of the level of firm-specific cleanup costs for sites identified through 1984.

Descriptive statistics and correlations among the three alternative measures of regulatory costs deflated by the level of chemical revenues are shown in Exhibit 9.2. Our goal is to isolate the underlying construct that is common to the three measures. To this end, we use a common factor analysis to decompose each individual measure into one (or more) factor(s) common to the individual measures of regulatory costs, and an additional factor that is unique to the specific measure alone. All the observations were subjected to factor analysis and one common factor

**Exhibit 9.2**
**Descriptive Statistics and Correlation Analysis of the Alternative**
**Measures of Regulating Costs**

### Panel A: Descriptive Statistics

| Variable | N | Mean | Std. Dev. | Median |
|---|---|---|---|---|
| TCN/CHEMREV | 51 | 0.0103 | 0.0329 | 0.0037 |
| TCRD/CHEMREV | 51 | 0.9283 | 5.8823 | 0.0813 |
| TACR/CHEMREV | 51 | 0.0183 | 0.0963 | 0.0255 |

### Panel B: Pearson Correlation Coefficients

Significance levels (basend on a two-tailed test) are shown in parentheses.

| | TCN/ CHEMREV | TCRD/ CHEMREV | TACR/ CHEMREV |
|---|---|---|---|
| TCN/CHEMREV | 1.000 | | |
| | (0.000) | | |
| TCRD/CHEMREV | 0.96806 | 1.000 | |
| | (0.0001) | (0.000) | |
| TACR/CHEMREV | 0.96282 | 0.99673 | 1.000 |
| | (0.0001) | (0.0001) | (0.000) |

TCN: The cumulative number of Superfund Notice Letters as of 1984.
TCRD: The total cost reported in the records of Decisions as of 1984 across all sites in the firm.
TACR: The allocated cost reported in the Records of Decisions as of 1984 summed across all sites based on an equal allocation of the total costs among all COMPU-STAT Potentially Responsible Parties.
CHEMREV: Chemical revenues in millions.

was found to explain the interrecorrelations among the three individual measures (Hartman, 1976). Exhibit 9.3 reports the results of the common factor analysis. One common factor appears to explain the interrecorrelations among the three variables, as the first eigenvalue alone exceeds the sum of the commonalities. The common factor is significantly and positively correlated with the three measures. A factor score is then computed for each firm as the index of regulatory cost (IRC).

### Measurement of the Size of the Environmental Exposure

The size of environmental exposure is measured by the logarithm of chemical revenues rather than total revenues or ratio of chemical revenues to total revenues. The judgment was that the magnitude of chemical revenues best defines the size of the environmental exposure. We argue, *ceteris paribus*, that firms with larger levels of chemical revenues face greater public pressure than firms with smaller levels of chemical revenues.

### Variables in the Cross-Sectional Analysis

The general cross-sectional model is described as follows:

$$EDI_j = a1 + a1 * IRC_j + a2 * LNCHEMREV_j$$

where:

$$
\begin{aligned}
EDI_j &= \text{Environmental disclosure index for firm } j. \\
IRC_j &= \text{Index of regulatory cost for firm } j. \\
LNCHEMREV_j &= \text{Logarithm of chemical revenues for firm } j.
\end{aligned}
$$

$EDI_j$ is obtained from the content analysis of each firm's 10-K report. $IRC_j$ is the factor score from the factor analysis of the three alternative measures of regulatory costs.

### RESULTS

Exhibit 9.4 presents descriptive statistics and correlation analysis of EDI, IRC, and LNCHEMREV. Results of the test of significance for the determinants of environmental disclosures are presented in Exhibit 9.5.

**Exhibit 9.3**
Factor Analysis

Initial Factor Method: Principal Components

Prior Communality Estimates: ONE

Eigenvalues of the Correlation Matrix: Total = 3, Average = 1

|  | 1 | 2 | 3 |
|---|---|---|---|
| Eigenvalue | 2.9518 | 0.0451 | 0.0031 |
| Difference | 2.9067 | 0.0421 |  |
| Proportion | 0.9839 | 0.0150 | 0.0010 |
| Cumulative | 0.9839 | 0.9990 | 1.0000 |

1 Factors will be retained by the NFACTOR criterion

Factor Pattern

|  | FACTOR1 |
|---|---|
| TCN | 0.98481 |
| TCRD | 0.99636 |
| TACR | 0.99461 |

Variance explained by each factor

FACTOR1

2.951815

**Exhibit 9.3** (continued)

Final Communality Estimates: Total = 2.951815

| TCN | TCRD | TACR |
|---|---|---|
| 0.969846 | 0.992726 | 0.989243 |

Scoring Coefficients Estimated by Regression

Squared Multiple Correlations of the Variables with each Factor

FACTOR1

1.000000

Standardized Scoring Coefficients

| | FACTOR1 |
|---|---|
| TCN | 0.33363 |
| TCRD | 0.33754 |
| TACR | 0.33695 |

TCN: The cumulative number of Superfund Notice Letters as of 1984.
TCRD: The total cost reported in the Records of Decisions as of 1984 across all sites for the firm.
TACR: The total cost reported in the Records of Decisions as of 1984 summed across all sites for the firm, based on an equal allocation.

**Exhibit 9.4**
**Descriptive Statistics and Correlation Analysis of Firm-Specific Variables**

**Panel A: Descriptive Statistics**

| Variable | N | Mean | Std. Dev. | Median | Minimum | Maximum |
|----------|----|---------|-----------|----------|---------|---------|
| EDI | 51 | 2.8113 | 1.4150 | 3 | 1.0000 | 5.0000 |
| IRC | 51 | 58.1930 | 69.6693 | 33.0505 | 0.0000 | 75.5013 |
| CHEMREV | 51 | 2588.59 | 1211.00 | 935.9800 | 0.0000 | 38419.6 |

**Panel B: Pearson Correlation Coefficients**

Significance levels (based on a two-tailed test).

|  | EDI | IRC | CHEMREV |
|---------|---------|---------|---------|
| EDI | 1.000 |  |  |
|  | 0.000 |  |  |
| IRC | 0.63866 | 1.000 |  |
|  | 0.0001 | 0.000 |  |
| CHEMREV | 0.44318 | 0.54373 | 1.000 |
|  | 0.0009 | 0.00001 | 0.000 |

EDI:  Environmental Disclosure Index
IRC:  Index of Regulatory Cost
CHEMREV: Chemical Revenues

**Exhibit 9.5**
**Results of Cross-Sectional Regression Model Investigating the**
**Determinants of Environmental Disclosure**

| Independent Variable* | Predicted Sign | |
|---|---|---|
| Intercept | | 0.0496 |
| t statistic | | 0.079 |
| p value | | 0.9376 |
| | | |
| IRC | + | 0.0085 |
| t statistic | | 3.644 |
| p value | | 0.0007 |
| | | |
| LNCHEMREV | + | 0.3079 |
| t statistic | | 2.985 |
| p value | | 0.004 |

Number of observations     51

Adjusted R - Squared         52.36%

F Statistic                          26.382

P value                             0. 0001

* IRC: Index of Regulatory Costs

Examination of the table reveals that both independent variables, the index of regulatory costs and the logarithm of chemical revenues, are in the direction hypothesized (positive) and both are statistically significant at the 0.001 level. In addition, the model is significant ($F = 26.382$, $p = 0.0001$) and explains 52.36 percent of the variation in environmental disclosures of these chemical firms. The results are consistent with both discretionary disclosure and legitimacy theory predictions for environmental disclosures.

## SUMMARY AND CONCLUSIONS

The discretionary disclosure thesis implies that the extent of discretionary disclosure is proportional to the amount of bad news. The corporate legitimacy thesis implies that the extent of discretionary disclosure is proportional to the level of exposure of the firm to the social/political climate. In the context of this study, the two hypotheses imply that the extent of environmental disclosures is proportional to regulatory costs and chemical revenues. The results of the study using data from a sample of fifty-one U.S. chemical firms confirmed the two hypotheses by showing that environmental disclosures included in the 10-K reports were positively related to an index of regulatory costs and the level of exposure to environmental risk as measured by the logarithm of chemical revenues. In addition to a verification of the discretionary disclosure and the corporate legitimacy theses, the results confirm earlier studies on the relationships between social disclosure and social performance. The lesson that can be derived by the profession is the need for adequate matching of the quality of social disclosure with the extent of social performance.

## NOTES

1. A. A. Ullmann, "Data in Search of a Theory: A Critical Examination of the Relationships among Social Performance, Social Disclosure, and Economic Performance of U.S. Firms," *Academy of Management Review* 10 (1985), pp. 540–557.

2. D. Patten, "Exposure, Legitimacy, and Social Disclosure," *Journal of Accounting and Public Policy* (1991), pp. 297–308.

3. D. Patten, "Intra-Industry Environmental Disclosures in Response to the Alaskan Oil Spill: A Note on Legitimacy Theory," *Accounting, Organizations and Society* (1992), p. 471–475.

4. W. Blacconiere and D. Patten, "Environmental Disclosures, Regulatory Costs, and Changes in Firm Value," *Journal of Accounting and Economics* 18 (1994), pp. 357–377.

5. W. F. Abbott and R. J. Monsen, "On the Measurement of Corporate Social Responsibility: Self-Reported Disclosure as a Method of Measuring Corporate Social Involvement," *Academy of Management Journal* 22 (1979), pp. 501–515.

6. E. H. Bowman and M. Haire, "A Strategic Posture toward Corporate Social Responsibility," *California Management Review* 18 (1975), pp. 49–58.

7. M. Freedman and B. Jaggi, "Pollution Disclosures, Pollution Performance and Economic Performance," *Omega* 10 (1982), pp. 167–176.

8. F. Fry and R. J. Hock, "Who Claims Responsibility? The Biggest and the Worst," *Business* 2 (1976), pp. 32–48.

9. R. W. Ingram and K. B. Frazier, "Environmental Performance and Corporate Disclosure," *Journal of Accounting Research* 18 (1980), pp. 614–622.

10. L. E. Preston and J. E. Post, *Private Management and Public Policy* (Englewood Cliffs, N.J.: Prentice-Hall, 1975).

11. J. Wiseman, "An Evaluation of Environmental Disclosures Made in Corporate Annual Reports," *Accounting, Organizations and Society* 7 (1982), pp. 53–63.

12. Ahmed Belkaoui and Philip G. Karpik, "Determinants of the Corporate Decision to Disclose Social Information," *Accounting, Auditing and Accounting* 2 (1989), pp. 36–51.

13. "How Business School Students Rate Corporations," *Business and Society Review* 2 (1972), pp. 20–21.

14. M. R. Moskowitz, "Choosing Socially Responsible Stocks," *Business and Society Review* 1 (1972), pp. 29–42.

15. R. Verrecchia, "Discretionary Disclosure," *Journal of Accounting and Economics* 5 (1983), pp. 179–194.

16. R. A. Dye, "Disclosure of Nonproprietary Information," *Journal of Accounting Research* 23 (1985), pp. 123–145.

17. M. N. Darrough and N. M. Stoughton, "Financial Disclosure in an Entry Game," *Journal of Accounting and Economics* 12 (1990), pp. 113–143.

18. A. Dontoh, "Voluntary Disclosure," *Journal of Accounting, Auditing and Finance* 4 (1989), pp. 480–511.

19. P. Newman and R. Sansing, "Disclosure Policies with Multiple Users," *Journal of Accounting Research* 31 (1993), pp. 92–112.

20. H. Schreuder and K. V. Ramanathan, "Accounting and Corporate Accountability: An Extended Comment," *Accounting, Organizations and Society* 9 (1984), pp. 409–416.

21. G. J. Benston, "Accounting and Corporate Accountability," *Accounting, Organizations and Society* 2 (1982), pp. 87–105.

## SELECTED READINGS

Abbott, W. F., and R. J. Monsen. "On the Measurement of Corporate Social Responsibility: Self-Reported Disclosure as a Method of Measuring Corporate Social Involvement." *Academy of Management Journal* 22 (1979), pp. 501–515.

Barth, M., M. McNichols, and G. Wilson. "Determinants of Firms' Decisions to Disclose and Accrue Information about Environmental Liabilities." Working Paper (Massachusetts Institute of Technology and Stanford University, 1995).

Belkaoui, Ahmed, and Philip G. Karpik. "Determinants of the Corporate Decision to Disclose Social Information." *Accounting, Auditing and Accountability* 2 (1989), pp. 36–51.

Benston, G. J. "Accounting and Corporate Accountability." *Accounting, Organizations and Society* 2 (1982), pp. 87–105.

Blacconiere, W., and D. Patten. "Environmental Disclosures, Regulatory Costs, and Changes in Firm Value." *Journal of Accounting and Economics* 18 (1994), pp. 357–377.

Bowman, E. H., and M. Haire. "A Strategic Posture toward Corporate Social Responsibility." *California Management Review* 18 (1975), pp. 49–58.

Darrough, M. N., and N. M. Stoughton. "Financial Disclosure in an Entry Game." *Journal of Accounting and Economics* 12 (1990), pp. 113–143.

Dontoh, A. "Voluntary Disclosure." *Journal of Accounting, Auditing and Finance* 4 (1989), pp. 480–511.

Dye, R. A. "Disclosure of Nonproprietary Information." *Journal of Accounting Research* 23 (1985), pp. 123–145.

Freedman, M., and B. Jaggi. "Pollution Disclosures, Pollution Performance and Economic Performance." *Omega* 10 (1982), pp. 167–176.

Fry, F., and R. J. Hock. "Who Claims Responsibility? The Biggest and the Worst." *Business* 2 (1976), pp. 32–48.

Guthrie, J., and L. Parker. "Corporate Social Disclosure Practice: A Comparative International Analysis." *Advances in Public Interest Accounting* 1 (1990), pp. 159–176.

Hartman, H. H. *Modern Factor Analysis*, 3rd ed. Chicago: University of Chicago, 1976.

"How Business School Students Rate Corporations." *Business and Society Review* 2 (1972), pp. 20–21.

Ingram, R. W., and K. B. Frazier. "Environmental Performance and Corporate Disclosure." *Journal of Accounting Research* 18 (1980), pp. 614–622.

Moskowitz, M. R. "Choosing Socially Responsible Stocks." *Business and Society Review* 1 (1972), pp. 29–42.

Newman, P., and R. Sansing. "Disclosure Policies with Multiple Users." *Journal of Accounting Research* 31 (1993), pp. 92–112.

Northcut, D. "Environmental Accounting Choices in Firms Subject to Superfund Cleanup Costs." Working Paper (Tucson: University of Arizona, 1995).

Patten, D. "Exposure, Legitimacy, and Social Disclosure." *Journal of Accounting and Public Policy* (1991), pp. 297–308.

———. "Intra-Industry Environmental Disclosures in Response to the Alaskan Oil Spill: A Note on Legitimacy Theory." *Accounting, Organizations and Society* 3 (1992), pp. 471–475.

Preston, L. E. "Analyzing Corporate Social Performance: Methods and Results." *Journal of Contemporary Business* 7 (1978), pp. 135–150.

Preston, L. E., and J. E. Post. *Private Management and Public Policy*. Englewood Cliffs, N.J.: Prentice-Hall, 1975.

Schreuder, H., and K. V. Ramanathan. "Accounting and Corporate Accountability: An Extended Comment." *Accounting, Organizations and Society* 9 (1984), pp. 409–416.

Ullmann, A. A. "Data in Search of a Theory: A Critical Examination of the Relationships among Social Performance, Social Disclosure, and Economic Performance of U.S. Firms." *Academy of Management Review* 10 (1985), pp. 540–557.

Verrecchia, R. "Discretionary Disclosure." *Journal of Accounting and Economics* 5 (1983), pp. 179–194.
Wagenhoffer, A. "Voluntary Disclosure with a Strategic Opponent." *Journal of Accounting and Economics* 12 (1990), pp. 341–363.
Wiseman, J. "An Evaluation of Environmental Disclosures Made in Corporate Annual Reports." *Accounting, Organizations and Society* 7 (1982), pp. 53–63.

# Index

**About the Author**

AHMED RIAHI-BELKAOUI is Professor of Accounting at the College of Business Administration, The University of Illinois–Chicago, and Chairman of the Cultural Studies and Accounting Research Committee, American Accounting Association (Internal Accounting Section). Riahi-Belkaoui is also a member of the editorial board of several professional journals and is the author of 24 previous Quorum books and coauthor of 3 more.

ISBN 1-56720-243-8

90000>

EAN

9 781567 202434

HARDCOVER BAR CODE